LIFE, FREEDOM AND WAR
Twentieth Century South Asia

LIFE, FREEDOM AND WAR

Twentieth Century South Asia

Edited by

Sho Kuwajima

Life, Freedom and War: Twentieth Century South Asia
Edited by Sho Kuwajima

First Published 2010

ISBN 978-93-5002-098-2

Published by
AAKAR BOOKS
28 E Pocket IV, Mayur Vihar Phase I, Delhi 110 091
Phone: 011-2279 5505 Telefax : 011-2279 5641
aakarbooks@gmail.com; www.aakarbooks..com

Composed by
Limited Colors, Delhi 110 092

Printed at
Mudrak, 30 A Patparganj, Delhi 110 091

Contents

Preface

This is a small collection of five papers. These papers were written in 2006 as a part of our larger joint work. Due to various reasons the original plan had to be given up. The papers mainly discuss the history and society in South Asia from the 1920 to the 1960s. The themes in these papers cover various aspects of political and social life in South Asia: nationalists and communists, social mobility among the lowest strata of the people, the impact of the Second World War on the life of the people, and women and children in particular, and nationalism and secularism in the thought of a Muslim political leader. However, one thing common among these papers is that all papers have tried to throw light on the less known aspects of the thought of prominent leaders or the less known part of the contemporary history of South Asia. In this sense, all of our authors shall be happy if this publication stimulates serious discussion on the themes presented here. A memoir of my contacts with my teachers, colleagues, friends and many unknown people in India in 1962–66 was added to facilitate the understanding of the relevance of the seemingly 'unsystematic' collection of these papers.

Virendra Nath Chattopadhyaya's name became known widely since it appeared in Jawaharlal Nehru's autobiography, in which he wrote about the meeting of the League against Imperialism and the role of Virendra Nath, who was not only active in political activities, but also helped many Indians who visited Europe. But the details of his life including his tragic death in Russia were not known to us till Nirodh K. Barooah's work appeared[1]. Surendra Gopal, who had been interested for long in the life of Virendra Nath, discussed his writings for *Inprecor* (*International Press Correspondence*), the organ of the Comintern, in 1930–31, which Barooah's work did not cover fully. He concluded that Chattopadhyaya never omitted facts, carefully collected evidence, and only in conclusion did he stick to the line laid down by the Comintern and remain loyal to the cause of the Soviet Union.

L.S. Vishwanath starts his paper with his observation that, except for a few sociologists, most students of Indian society seem to have neglected B.R. Ambedkar's writings on the Hindu caste system, Hinduism and Buddhism. Ambedkar was not only active throughout his life serving the oppressed Dalits, but was also a serious student of India's economy and society. In this paper, Vishwanath examines Ambedkar's ideas in the light of the research findings of sociologists and historians, including his own findings in his work on the social history of colonial Gujarat. For instance, in his Colombia seminar paper in 1916, Ambedkar says that whatever open door character caste may have had as class in the past, it was 'lost', and classes became self-enclosed units called 'castes'. The main reason was the endogamous rule. Vishwanath finds that endogamous rule was not rigidly followed among quite a few castes. However, he concludes that, at that early stage, Ambedkar seems open to suggestions on castes, but later, due to his bitter experiences, there was a hardening of position.

In 1942 many people were evacuated from Chennai to safer places to escape the Japanese bombing, and Chennai became a ghost city[2]. Rajam Krishnan, a prominent Tamil

1 Barooah, Nirodh K. 2004. *Chatto—The Life and Times of an Indian Anti-Imperialist in Europe*, New Delhi: Oxford University Press.

2 Ramabhadran, "In the shadow of World War", *The Hindu*, 16 August 1992.

writer, vividly describes how the burdens of a big family were imposed on her shoulder on account of the war. This paper shows that the exodus of the people from Chennai, as well as Burma and their deaths along the way, and the problem of rehabilitating people who could fortunately reach South India, were the result of the Japanese air-raid in southeast and south Asia. Unarmed people—women in particular suffered in India, too. In this paper, the appearance of S.R. Ranganathan, a well-known library scientist, in the classroom as an Education Officer, and the lonely death of a revolutionary who fought for Indian freedom with arms, are unforgettable scenes.

This is also a story of the birth of a writer who came to express her idea in the literary world under the extremely difficult wartime and post-war conditions. In this connection, Rajam Krishnan writes that she started writing her ideas on the backside of the bills which her mother-in-law brought with daily goods from the market. This was just what I experienced during the Second World War. Due to an extreme shortage of paper, we used as our 'notebooks' the backside of the unused bills presented by the mother of a classmate.

A paper on the American air raid, Tokyo, 9–10 March 1945, which killed one lakh people in one night, also shows that, in the war, children as well as women suffered a lot, and children had to decide on their own how to act at this critical moment of history. Rajam Krishnan's essay and this one should be read as a set to find out how the burden of the war had to be carried primarily by the women and children, while Japan was busy imposing difficulties on the people of Asia. Though this paper is not specifically related to South Asian Studies, it shows that this wartime experience promoted some of our generation in Japan to make a new image of Asia in the context of the Indian foreign policy in the 1950s which took the leading role in the Korean and

Vietnamese armistice, however different an interpretation may have appeared on the policy in later years.

Abul Hashim, the General Secretary of the Bengal Muslim League in 1943–47, is a less known political leader and thinker despite his role in vitalizing the Muslim League organizations in Bengal from 1943 to 1945. Even in Bengal he has attracted less attention in comparison with Fazlul Huq and H.S. Suhrawardy. What was in my mind since the 1960s was why he and his followers were once called the 'progressives' or the 'left', why Hashim's idea was shared by the Muslim educated youth, and why they seemed to have disappeared from the political scene in the critical pre-partition period. Here, I tried to find out the reason with limited materials and findings.

I thank Mr. K.K. Saxena of Aakar Books for his prompt, but careful support in bringing out our work in its present form.

Lastly, I would like to express my thanks to Mr. S. Ansari, former Chief Librarian, Dr. Zakir Husain Library, Jamia Millia Islamia, New Delhi, and a good friend since 1962, who kindly helped a lot in the publication of this small work.

Sho Kuwajima

1

Pen for Pistol: Virendra Nath Chattopadhyaya and the League Against Imperialism

Surendra Gopal

Virendra Nath Chattopadhyaya was among those Indian revolutionaries who left their motherland to fight for its independence against British domination in the first decade of the last century. He never returned; he lost his life to Soviet bullets in Leningrad in the late 1930s. He spent the three decades fighting for India's freedom successively in London (1902–1910), Paris (1910–14), Berlin (1914–1931), Moscow (1931–1933) and Leningrad (now St. Petersburg) (1933–37).

During his prolonged residence in Berlin, he first acted as coordinator between Indian patriots and the German Government, keen to promote an Indian upsurge while the First World War was raging. After Germany lost the war, Chattopadhyaya remained in Berlin, helping Indian students and visitors to Germany and promoting the cause of Indian independence in Central Europe.

In 1926, Chattopadhyaya was asked to assist Muenzenberg, the Secretary of, the German Communist Party, in organizing a Conference named as the League against Cruelties and Opression in the Colonies, scheduled to be held at Brussels. He was given this responsibility as he had persuaded, Jawaharlal Nehru to participate as a nominee of the Indian National Congress, then in the vanguard for the fight for Indian independence.

When the Congress began, the delegates decided to make it a permanent body; it was renamed as the League Against Imperialism and for National Independence.[1] Muenzenberg, impressed by the multi-lingual ability of Chatto and his organizing skill, asked him to look after the day-to-day working of the Secretariat. Chattopadhyaya used this new opportunity to plead more actively for the cause of Indian freedom in the journal *Inprecor* (*International Press Correspondence*), the mouthpiece of Comintern.

I

The present paper examines the writings of Chatto, as they appeared in this journal till he left for the Soviet Union. His criticism of Great Britain was on the lines suggested by Comintern. He also took care that his writings should not sour relations between the Soviet Union and Great Britain, since the compulsion of international politics forced the former to woo the latter despite its capitalist system and alliance with other imperial powers.

Let us briefly trace the beginnings of Chattopadhyaya's involvement with Indian revolutionaries and their activities.

Virendra Nath Chattopadhyaya, son of Dr. Aghore Nath Chattopadhyaya, a distinguished educationist of the nineteenth century, was the younger brother of Smt. Sarojini Naidu, a valiant freedom fighter. He arrived in England in 1902 to write his ICS examination but became involved in revolutionary activities along with freedom fighters such as Shyamji Krishna Varma, Madam Bhikhaiji Cama, S.S. Rana, V.D. Savarkar, V.V.S. Aiyar, etc.

Following the assassination of Lt. Col. Wylie on 1 July 1909 by Madanlal Dhingra, an Indian student, the UK government adopted repressive measures towards Indian revolutionaries. After the Government arrested Savarkar, Indian activists were forced to quit London in 1910. Most of them, including Chattopadhyaya, took refuge in Paris and carried on their campaign against British rule in India. But they were compelled to shift again after the First World War broke out in 1914.

In this war, France and Great Britain became allies against Wilhelmite Germany. France, in order to please its ally Great Britain, outlawed and banned Indian revolutionary activities on its soil. Madam Cama and S.R. Rana were interned; Shyamji Varma shifted to Geneva, and Chattopadhyaya crossed over to Germany.

Chattopadhyaya's decision was fortunate: Germany was willing to welcome and support Indian patriots so as to weaken British war efforts by inciting uprisings on the Indian subcontinent. German strategy was three fold: (i) extend diplomatic, financial and military support to Indian revolutionaries gathered in Berlin, (ii) help Indians who had been organized under the banner of the Ghadar Party in the USA to promote armed up risings in India, and (iii) finally, ensure the installation of a Provisional Government of Free India in Kabul on the borders of India under Raja Mahendra Pratap so as to keep the English in India on tenter-hooks with the threat of a possible tribal attack from across the northwestern borders of India.

In order to put their designs into practice, the Indian patriots and the German government formed the Indian Independence Committee in Berlin with Virendra Nath Chattopadhyaya as its principal member. He coordinated the activities of Indian revolutionaries based in Europe throughout the war and remained the principal link of Indians with the German Foreign Office.[2]

Indian revolutionaries failed to achieve their objective as Germany suffered defeat in the First World War and monarchy was replaced by a republic. India remained subject to Great Britain. Chattopadhyaya continued to live in Germany as the new German Republic was not hostile to revolutionaries and the British would not allow him to return to India. In the changed circumstances, the German government was no longer as supportive of Indian patriots as it was during the war, but it permitted them to stay back and actively work for the independence of their country. Meanwhile, the international situation had undergone a sea change. The Soviet Union had come into existence. Lenin and other Soviet leaders had formed the Comintern or Third International to advance the cause of Marxism and promote a world revolution against colonialism and imperialism. The Soviets were not unmindful of the presence of Indian revolutionaries in Germany. They decided to seek the cooperation of Indian revolutionaries to further the cause of proletariat revolution. They had already invited M.N. Roy, who was staying in Mexico. Chattopadhyaya and other Indian revolutionaries, such as Bhupendra Nath Dutta, Pandurang Khankhoje, and others. were now invited to attend the third Congress of Comintern in Moscow.

During the deliberations of the Comintern, Lenin and Comintern made M.N. Roy in charge of Indian affairs. He remained in this position from 1919 to 1928. Indians returned to Berlin.

II

This was the beginning of Chattopadhyaya's association with the Comintern and the Communists. In the early years he was treated by the Comintern as a sympathizer and was hardly given any meaningful political responsibility.

In the absence of any worthwhile political activity, Chattopadhyaya concentrated on sociocultural work among Indians, even though he was penniless and hunted by the British intelligence agents. He acted as friend, philosopher and guide to all Indians who arrived in or passed through

Berlin. Though not a member of the Communist Party, he remained in touch with M.N. Roy, who had made Berlin his base for propagating the ideals and policies of Comintern through journals he brought out with the financial support of the Comintern and the Soviet Union. Chattopadhyaya's unalloyed patriotism and devotion to the cause of Indian independence won him the respect of leaders of the Indian National Congress such as Jawaharlal Nehru and Rajendra Prasad, both of whom met him during their visit to Berlin.

Undoubtedly, among Indians residing in Berlin in the 1920s, Chattopadhyaya stood out for his intellectual sharpness and dedication to the cause of Indian independence. When, in 1927 at Brussels Comintern decided to hold a meeting of the Oppressed people, where a huge delegation of Indian National Congress led by Jawaharlal Nehru was expected to be present, they decided to associate Chattopadhyaya with it. He would be a symbol of cosmopolitanism of the Comintern and its deep concern for the people of the colonies. The meet decided to establish the League Against Imperialism (LAI) to promote the cause of anti-colonialism anti-imperialism. Chattopadhyaya had impressed the organizers of the meeting with his zeal and efficient working. He was invited to assist its Secretary, Muenzenberg, and was given the status of Joint Secretary. Muenzenberg was also the Secretary of the German Communist Party.[3]

The new responsibility seemed to have reinvigorated Chattopadhyaya, who now devoted himself heart and soul to the new organization so that it successfully carried out the fight against imperialism and motivated the people of the colonies to revolt against their imperialist rulers. During this period, Chatto's association with LAI became more intense; he was holding conferences and enlisting support for its activities; he was expanding the scope of its activities.

Chattopadhyaya was closely associated with its organizational functions; he was coordinating with the leaders of the freedom struggle now being waged in the colonies in different parts of the world. He helped in the organisation of second Congress of the League, held at Frankfurt on the Maine in July 1929.[4]

It was in the course of his work with the LAI that Chatto's abilities as a journalist received the acclaim of his co-workers.

In 1928, the League asked him to edit *Anti-Imperialist Review* (published from Berlin), an organ of the League. But his journalistic talents really came to the forefront when he became associated with *Inprecor* (*International Press Correspondence*), published since 1921 as the mouthpiece of Comintern.

It seems that Muenzenberg was convinced of the ability of Chattopadhyaya as a journalist to put across the prime concerns of the League convincingly to the leaders; he virtually allowed him to run this weekly journal in 1930 and 1931. During his membership of the League, Chattopadhyaya had become a member of the Communist Party. This also enhanced the faith of the top echelons of the Comintern in him. They were sure that he would faithfully carry out Diktats, especially the line laid down by Sixth Congress of Comintern, held at Moscow in 1928. The Comintern, at this point of time, was badly in need of an Indian leader to counteract M.N. Roy who had been expelled from the Party in 1928 and was now hobnobbing with the leaders of the Indian National Congress.

Chattopadhyaya found a welcome instrument in the journal *Inprecor*, which was also made the organ of the League to express his anti-British and anti-capitalist views, and to propagate the ideology of anti-racism, anti-colonialism and to uphold the policies of the Bolshevik regime of the Soviet Union.

III

In the present paper, Chattopadhyaya's contributions published in the *Inprecor* have been examined; the conclusion is that although espousing the ideology of the League, Chattopadhyaya's primary concern remained the cause of freedom struggle going on in India for ousting the English domination.

The *Inprecor* was published in several languages; Chattopadhyaya was associated primarily with the English edition, which had a worldwide circulation.

The Sixth Congress of Comintern had termed all socialists, the supporters of Second International, as imperialist agents; it criticised them and dubbed all their non-Communist allies as enemies of the proletariat. In India, the Comintern mounted its attack on the Indian National Congress, which was leading the struggle against the British, and its top leaders such as Gandhi, Nehru, Patel, etc. In 1929, the League had already begun criticising the role of Gandhi and the Indian National Congress in India's freedom struggle. Comintern's attitude was made clear by O.W. Kuusinen who exhorted Indians to carry out a determined fight against the Indian National Congress.[5]

Chattopadhyaya criticised, in writing, M.N. Roy, whom not long ago, he was requesting to sponsor his application for the membership of the Communist Party.

Even while affirming his loyalty to the Communist Party and the Comintern, Chattopadhyaya continued to espouse the cause of India's independence, the cause that was most dear to him. Of course, he insisted that to attain independence, Indians had to follow the path laid down in the resolutions of the Sixth Congress of the Comintern in 1928 and Indians had to abide by its judgements on strategies to be followed from time to time.

Throughout the year 1930, Chattopadhyaya wrote regularly on the Indian situation, so as to draw the world's attention to the fight being waged in India. The main emphasis of these articles was to show the growing militancy of the labour movement in the country. He scathingly criticised any political party, which denied primacy to the proletariat in the freedom struggle and, instead of armed resistance, pleaded for a negotiated settlement with the foreigners. It was this point of view that made Chattopadhyaya write a front page article entitled, 'The Indian Railway Strike', and warned them against the right-wing 'deviationists' including Jawaharlal Nehru, the then President of the Indian National Congress who had suggested that the dispute be referred to an arbitration board.[6] His ire against Nehru and the Indian National Congress rose in proportion to increase in their popularity in India. He was keen to warn the Indian leaders that all was not well with the Indian society. For this purpose, he published another article in the same issue on unemployment among the educated middle classes in india. He wanted to highlight the growing all round discontent in the country among the young and educated sections; he felt this would prepare the ground for the outbreak of an armed rebellion. Partly his analysis of the causes was correct.

He had put the blame squarely on the education system promoted by the government which was 'of a more or less literary character, no attention being paid to industrial, technical or agricultural subjects'.[7] To lend authenticity to his conclusion, he reported that the Bengal Unemployed Youth Union had decided to hold 'Unemployment Day' on 6 March 1930 with demonstrations, public meetings, et cetera.[8] Chattopadhyaya had failed to suggest an alternative.

Throughout the year he harped on the theme that discontent was rising in the country. He was partly correct because Gandhi was conducting the Civil Disobedience

Movement and had started the Salt Satyagraha; the Indian masses had given a positive response to his call. But in Chatto's view (consistent with the line laid by the Comintern), the Gandhian movement was bereft of any significance for Indian polity.

IV

His obsession with the so-called discontent in the Indian society was reflected in the article 'The Revolutionary Situation in India', published on the front page in the issue of 30 April 1930. He was referring to public demonstrations held against the British in the city of Peshawar, a few miles from Afghanistan, which was described by him as 'an indispensable point of advance in military operations against that country and the Soviet Russia.'[9] He took it as a good omen 'that in the operations against the "rebels" the British Government has used no Indian troops except the Gorkhas.' For him, it meant that the loyalty of Sikh troops was suspect in British eyes and the coercive power of imperialism was declining. He rated it as a plus point for the 'imminent' success of the 'imminent' Indian revolution. He said 'It may be prophesied with considerable certainty that Sikh troops will not be relied upon by the Government and that as the revolutionary movement assumes a proletarian character they will probably join the revolution.' In hindsight, it appears that Chattopadhyaya was hasty in his assessment. He was in no position to feel the pulse of the people. He was drawing general conclusions from isolated events. This tendency persisted.

Chattopadhyaya convinced himself that growing trade union militancy and activities and 'the growth of strike movement among workers' in India augured well for its anti-imperialist struggle. To prove his point, he appovingly referred to the Chittagong rebels who had set fire to the arsenal.[10] He was referring to the raid on the Chittagong armoury led by Surya Sen. He felt that armed struggle was the most effective means for attaining independence. He refused to see any wisdom among those Indian leaders who disagreed with him. He, therefore, bitterly criticised the moderates in Indian politics and called Tej Bahadur Sapru as 'Lord Irwin's agent'. Tej Bahadur Sapru was mediating between the Viceroy Lord Irwin and the leaders of the Indian National Congress. Henceforth, he indiscriminately criticised Congress and moderate leadership in India.

However, it must be said to the credit of Chattopadhyaya that in spite of using general terms for criticising the non-Communist political leaders and their politics, Chattopadhyaya was able to detect the growing Hindu-Muslim divide in politics. To buttress his point, he cites the example of Hindu Mahasabha and the Muslim League under Mohammed Ali electing representatives for attending the scheduled Round Table Conference to 'protect' Hindu and Muslim 'interests' respectively. To him, these instances showed, 'intimate connection between religion and imperialism.' But he did not attempt to find out the real cause of the chasm between the Hindus and the Muslims. Instead of locating intrinsic causes for this malady in the Indian body politic, he took the easy path and put the blame squarely on the shoulders of the alien government.

Chattopadhaya was unable to realize that his assessment of the Indian situation was based on a narrow view of Indian society and polity. He agreed with *The Workers Weekly* that 'the growing strength of the Indian revolutionary movement' had 'gone far beyond Gandhi'. This was a premature conclusion; if any leader was obeyed by the masses, it was Gandhi. Chattopadhyaya was simply echoing the tone set by the Comintern. He called upon the Indian Communist Party to 'give a clear direction to the movement.'[11] He failed to realize that the Indian Communist Party was still in the process of formation and had only pockets of influence in certain urban areas. It was in no position to lead the political struggle going on in India; Chattopadhyaya, in line with the Comintern, had an exaggerated assessment of the role and strength of the Indian Communist Party.

In the next issue of *Inprecor* (8 May 1930), Chattopadhyaya was back with his analysis of the Indian situation in another front page article entitled 'Revolutionary Development in India, Gandhi's Arrest'. He expressed his happiness that the masses were out in the streets following Gandhi's call for Salt Satyagrah and everywhere the Government had to take recourse to repression to contain the movement. The piece presents a brief but comprehensive analysis of the socio-economic and political situation of the country and an assessment of the indigenous industrial bourgeoisie, the landowners, the propertied classes, the peasants, the soldiers and the middle class. His conclusion was optimistic. 'It may therefore be confidently expected that the movement of the workers and the peasants will grow in intensity and be carried on under revolutionary slogans.'[12]

In conformity with the party line, Chattopadhyaya now started denouncing socialist parties though he still supported the cause of Indian Independence.

In the 22 May 1930 issue of *Inprecor*, his front-page article, 'India's Fight for Independence and the Second International', sought to demolish the faith of some Indians who hoped that the Labour Government in London led by Ramsay MacDonald would promote the Indian cause. He also wanted to show MacDonald's double-facedness: while promoting Indian hopes MacDonald was also defending colonialism under socialist regime.

In order to debunk those who pinned hopes on the good intentions of the Labour Government, Chattopadhyaya traced the history of the Second International from 1891 onward. The Social Democrat H. M. Hyndman, along with one Indian Sanyal[13] who had denounced the British exploitation of India and later on pulished several articles on this topic, had eventually become an ardent supporter of British naval expansion. Chattopadhyaya went into the history of socialist thought.

At the Socialist Congress at Paris (23-27 September 1900), the Dutch Van Kol formulated a theory, which could be interpreted 'as a socialist colonial policy with a civilising mission.'[14] This theme was taken up by Ramsay MacDonald at Stuttgart in 1907 when he voted for a resolution on the colonial question which stated: 'But it does not reject on principle and for all time every colonial policy, as this may have a civilising influence under a socialist regime.'[15]

It was in accordance with this spirit that even though the Socialists at the Brussels Congress in 1928 supported 'the endeavours of the Indian people to attain full self-Government', they avoided the word independence.[16] Chattopadhyaya's bitter critcism of socialists simply expressed the Comintern's thinking that there was no half-way house between Communism and Capitalism. In accordance with the decision of Comintern, he also took pains to justify the conviction that only the Revolutionary Marxist path would lead to independence.

V

Nevertheless, despite his strongly held views on the means to attain independence, differing sharply from popular Indian leaders, Chattopadhyaya ceaselessly spoke from all international fora in favour of India's freedom. As a result, he tried his best to follow closely political developments in the country. This is evident from his article entitled 'The Indian Revolution and the Nationalist Leaders'. Chattopadhyaya quoted excerpts from the speeches of Congress leaders who, despite the fact that the Congress had adopted a resolution for full independence, still continued to say 'if without any further delay India is offered complete responsible government within the British Commonwealth of nations, she would be prepared to accept it, and perhaps such responsible government is more to her advantage than isolated independence.'[17] In this article, he again asserted that there was a section of Muslims who did not support the call for India's independence. He pointed to Mohammad Ali, who while 'clamouring for the independence of Arabian Countries,' had distanced himself from the call for India's independence.[18]

Another report in the same issue concerns a meeting called by the League at Berlin on 10 May 1930 to express support for the cause of Indian independence. It was jointly chaired by Muenzenberg and Chattopadhyaya. The latter also delivered the political report. In the meeting it was decided to conduct an international campaign under the following slogans: 'Hands off India,' 'No soldiers and arms for India,' 'Withdrawal of the English Troops and Officials from India,' 'Not Pacifism and National Reformism; Only the Revolutionary Struggle of the Masses is the Way to India's Independence', 'Release the Meerut Prisoners!', 'Link up the Indian Struggle of the Revolutionary Proletariat and of the Peasantry in All Countries!' At the same meeting, a delegation was formed consisting of representatives from England, Holland, Czechoslovakia, Germany, France and the Balkans to visit India and report on the situation.[19] Chattopadhyaya's great service lay in the fact that he was trying to draw international attention to Indian struggle for freedom and to enlist support of all the anti-colonial elements.

The *Inprecor* of 28 May 1930 carried a front page article by Chttopadhyaya on the Indian situation entitled 'Further Intensification of the Fight in India, 'wherein he showed that, contrary to British government announcements, the Civil Disobedience Movement, instead of slackening, was 'spreading among large and larger sections of the population. There is an all round increase in the activities of the District and the Village Congress Committees, of the Workers' Union, of the Workers' and Peasants' Parties, of the nationalist terrorist organizations, of school and college students and of ex-soldiers of the Indian Army.[20] He especially praised the twenty-three freedom fighters of Sholapur (in Maharashtra) who had been sentenced to various terms of imprisonment by the Court Martial administration.

He also noted the success of the 'Red Shirts' movement in Peshawar and its spread among the tribes on India's northwest frontier.[21] He appreciated the importance of the strike of dock workers of Rangoon in Burma (then a part of India) for it would contribute to the success of freedom movement in India.[22]

The acts of heroic resistance in isolated pockets in India fired Chattopadhyaya's imagination. He concluded that the revolution was round the corner and the expulsion of the British was imminent. He felt his conclusion was justified when he reassessed the role of Muslims in India's freedom struggle. In his short essay 'The Indian Mohammedans and the Revolutionary Movement', he put forward the thesis that 'with the emergence of the class-line in the struggle, the religious differences that had been skilfully (*sic*) exploited for years together by the feudal and bourgeois leaders in their own interests and in the service of imperialism have ceased to be any longer effective'. He cited several instances of Muslim participation in the freedom struggle, especially in tribal areas and in the Punjab. He concluded, 'we realise that in the Punjab we have come one step nearer to the agrarian revolution.'[23] But the realist in him also perceived the contradictions in the role of certain important Muslim leaders such as Maulana Shaukat Ali and Mohammad Ali, who, while continuing to advocate independence for the Arab countries, still entertained reservations about Indian independence. He admitted their popularity among Muslim masses because their meetings in Bombay and Madras were attended by 1,00,000 people.[24] He was so much seized with the idea of Indian independence that he chose to ignore the contradictions in Muslim politics.

Chattopadhyaya had come to the conclusion that, 'the question of Muslims as a separate community does not arise in the case of the *Industrial Workers* (emphasis added), among whom economic and political factors alone count. 'The attempt to create "Muslim" unions has failed. It is these industrial workers that are playing an important role in the religious illusions that are still strong among the peasantry.'[25]

In India, the proletariat as a class was still in its formative stage. Morover, Indian cultural ethos also had their impact on the working class who could not conceive of a total break with its rural moorings and joint family system. As a result, neither numerically nor ideologically was it in a position to unleash a revolutionary movement.

By now Chatto had imbibed the Marxist view of history. He had convinced himself of the seminal role of economic factors in the development of a political situation. He also appreciated the crucial role of the industrial proletariat in bringing about societal and political changes. This is well reflected in his essay on 'May Day in India',[26] where he describes celebrations held on the first of May in different parts of India. He pointed out that the revolutionary monthly magazine, the *Kirti*, published from Amritsar had issued 'a May number' in Urdu and Gurmukhi containning splendid articles on May Day, on Marx, Lenin, Liebknecht and Rosa Luxemurg.'[27] He commented that the best demonstrations took place in Bombay, the city of revolutionary textile and railway workers and the most advanced section of the Indian proletariat.[28]

VI

Chattopadhyaya was now engrossed with the events taking placed in India, especially those having significance for the ongoing freedom movement. His piece, 'On the Situation in India' commended the intensification of the movement among the tribes on the northwest frontier of the country against the British: 'the tribe people did not give up despite destructive bombing by some 180 aerolanes.'[29] He pointed out that 'these tribes are not committing raids on Indian villages, as they had done in previous years, but have joined the Indian movement of national liberation.'[30] Though heaping scathing criticism on Congress leaders, he noted, 'But the no-rent campaign has spread to the United Provinces, Behar, Orissa and Bengal.'[31]

Chattopadhyaya remained deeply concerned with the tribal revolt on the northwest frontier of India, which was being ruthlessly suppressed by the British. Of course, a major motive for reporting British militay operations in this theatre was to mobilise world public opinion, because, as he put it, 'the objective ... is the occupation of the frontier of the Soviet Union.'[32] He debunked British insinuations that 'Soviet Russia is financing and arming the frontier tribes.'[33]

Chattopadhyaya while belittling the role of the Congress in the Indian freedom movement accepted its positive contributions. The tragedy of the left movement in India, is from the very beginning it failed to assess correctly the role of non-left forces in India's fight against colonialism and imperialism. The diktats of Comintern were responsible for this aberration.

There is a feeling that Chatto himself had some doubts about the position he had adopted in analyzing Indian situation. Otherwise he would not have tried to justify his position on India as consistent with the proclaimed objectives of the Sixth Congress of Comintern. For this he published a series of three articles by Radek, entitled 'Problems of the Revolution in India' in consecutive issues.

Radek contended that 'the industrial development of India except during the war is proceeding very slowly ... the destructive influence of British imperialism upon Indian economics, evidenced in the economic impoverishment of the Indian village and in the ceaseless additions to the army of the superfluous of dozens of millions of pauperized peasants, who found no place in industry, is developing more rapidly than the process of the industrialization of India.'[34] He further argued, 'The solution of Dominion Status for India, that is the placing India in the same position as Canada, Australia, and south America (sic) is simply utopian.'[35] Proceeding further, Radek noted, 'Independent rule, a future of free people—this imperialism will never voluntarily yield to the national bourgeoisie.'[36] He was emphatic, 'The struggle against the national reformists, the struggle against Gandhism, is no less important a prerequisite for the victory of the Indian revolution than the struggle against English Imperialism.'[37] He laid down that 'the aim of the revolutionary movement can only be socialism, and this can be realised by the seizure of power by the working class.'[38] Radek asserted that, 'The movement is beginning to get beyond the control of the national reformists. The national-revolutionary camp must place itself at its head'.[39]

Chatto's aim in publishing Radek's article appeared to give wide publicity to the Comintern line which was expected to be adhered to by all true Communists. It was a call to Indian revolutionaries that they must simultaneously fight imperialism and Gandhism; they should win freedom and not negotiate for it. By impeding industrialization of India, the Labour Government (of England) was not allowing proper environment for the growth of the freedom movement. Finally, the Comintern aimed at publicizing its views on all important events taking place in India so that the Indian 'revolutionaries' knew what position to take.

This was apparent when Chattopadhyaya wrote a front page article on the Simon Commission, which had visited India to recommend new constitutional reforms. The opening sentence read,

> Whenever British imperialism finds itself in difficulties in any of the areas exploited and plundered by it, or whenever it is forced to expand its social basis of imperialist rule in order to obtain a wider native cooperation in its machinery of exploitation and its war of aggression, it resorts to the appointment of 'Royal Commission' which go out to 'investigate' the situation 'impartially' and then make recommendation of "reforms" to his Majesty's Government.[40]

Students of constitutional history of British India would instantly realize the veracity of this statement of Chattopadhyaya.

He then went on to point out the contradictions in its recommendations. He felt that although the Report emphasized religious differences, it admitted that 'operations of large scale industry' bring together men of different castes and religions 'in the mills and mines,' where these differences do not exist.[41] This might have gladdened Chattopadhyaya, but the reality was different.

Chattopadhyaya was equally concerned with the continuing repression of tribes on the northwest frontier of India by the British because he felt that as opposed to the Tsarist times when British feared 'Russian menace', it was now the Soviet Russia which had to 'safeguard herself against the British menace.'[42] Maybe history had taken an about turn. In place of Russophobia, Anglophobia was now a part of Central Asian history. For a Communist and one associated with Comintern, the safety of the Soviet Union against imperialist intrigues, both perceived and imagined, was a major concern.

As is by now evident, Chattopadhyaya continued to comment upon the Indian political situation week after week in the pages of *Inprecor*. Despite the Marxist clichés he employed, his analysis was sometimes acute and penetrating. For example, in one of his pieces he wrote, 'A new feature of the movement is the increasing refusal of the Indian police to open fire upon Demonstrators. The Congress Committees are making special propaganda to persuade them to join the struggle for freedom.'[43] He supported his statement by citing a number of instances of refusal by policemen to fire upon these demonstrations of their compatriots.

While Chattopadhyaya admitted that Congress had succeeded in creating an anti-British mood in the country, he disliked the methods employed by the Indian Boycott Movement. He dubbed it as a return to 'retrograde medieval methods' and insisted that 'the whole of the movement for the boycott of British goods is proving to be highly profitable weapon in the hands of the Indian capitalists.'[44] Honesty prevailed. He furnished a number of instances to buttress his conclusions.

He admitted that the boycott movement had created an adverse impact on Lancashire and on German, Japanese and French industries.[45] He noted, 'The American bourgeoisie has (sic) declared its 'sympathy for the Indian movement,' while USA manufacturers have obtained a large number of orders from India for goods that had hitherto been imported from Great Britain.'[46] Capitalists compete for increasing their profit irrespective of ideological identity.

Chattopadhyaya's essays or comments on India week after week touched topics primarily of interest to political activists. One example is his repeated comments on the report of the Simon Commission, set up to suggest constitutional changes in India by the imperial government. When the second volume of the report of the Simon

Commission embodying concrete proposals for constitutional changes in India came out on 25 June 1930, he carefully dissected it and had no hesitation in declaring, 'The recommendations for "constitutional changes" ... constitute an enormous strengthening of imperialist domination.'[47] He further noted, 'the imperial Government has vastly increased its power and capacity of creating internal strife. By the maintenance of the communal electorates the religious riots that imperialist intrigue has hitherto provoked will now be multiplied ...'[48]

He returned to the report of the Simon Commission in subsequent issues of *Inprecor*. He noted, 'They [the British Government] have transferred political initiative into the hands of the Government and forced bourgeois politicians to concentrate all their energies on discussing the conditions of participation in the Round Table Conference.' On the basis of analysis he concluded, '... it is clear that the betrayal of the movement of independence is being organised by the Congress and Labour Reformist Leaders.'[49]

He was prophetic. He could grasp that politically Hindus and Muslims were drifting apart. The 1930s witnessed the clear articulation of Muslim demand of a separate homeland, Pakistan, which, in the 1940s led to the division of India. Chattopadhyaya voiced his concern.

VII

His piece, 'The Role of English-"Muslims" in the Colonies'[50] denounced Englishmen who had accepted Islam or Hinduism 'as supporters if not ... direct agents of British imperialist penetration and "intelligence" in Islamic and other countries.' He cited the example of Lord Headly who had converted to Islam and of Annie Besant in India who behaved like 'a Hindu by "conviction" and living and dressing as a Hindu, ... has acquired power and popularity among the upper class of Hindus, ...'[51]

From now onwards he was preoccupied with two problems: Hindu-Muslim question and the role of the governing British Labour Party. His subsequent essays mainly focus on these major issues.

The last issue of *Inprecor* of the year 1930 carried and overall assessment of the work done at the Round Table Conference during the previous six weeks. Chattopadhyaya had no hesitation in saying,

> The 'enormous difficulties' of granting "responsible self-government" to India are being deliberately illustrated by the conflict that has been taking place between the Muslims and Hindus at the Conference... But the Hindu–Muslim question does not exist outside the ranks of the job-hunters. The workers and peasants are united in their economic and political demands, and as soon as they free themselves completely from the 'guidance' of their bourgeois and petty bourgeois leaders, the whole 'federal Union' of the imperialists and their agents will be annihilated and the true Federal Republic of the Workers and Peasants established.'[52]

Little did Chattopadhyaya realise that the chasm between the Hindus and the Muslims was widening and not narrowing! He was unable to appreciate the deep divide existing between the Hindu and Muslim politicians. He was carried away by the Marxist rhetoric so much that he glossed over the irreconcilable elements between the two communities.

In the issue of 14 August 1930 under the pseudonym V. Ch., Chattopadhyaya wrote another article 'The I.L.P. Hypocrites and India.' His contention was that for 'imperialism and bourgeois nationalism to have come to a compromise after a few preliminary skirmishes, and it is these "left wing" parties on both sides that are working to bring about the agreement for the joint control and exploitation of the masses and the suppression of the revolutionary movement.'[53] He denounced Labourites such as Fenner Brockway, H.W. Nevinson, Brailsford, etc., who all sympathized with the Indian cause as people whose '...talk about "full self government", and "independence" is merely a bait with which to draw the Indian leaders into the imperialist net.' His final verdict was, 'The I.L.P. is in fact the left wing of British imperialism.'[54] Chattopadhyaya's aversion to British Labour Party leaders was a reflection of Comintern's declared hostility to socialists connected with the Second International.

Chattopadhyaya's hatred for the non-Communist left was reflected in his condemnation of the policies of the Indian National Congress. Chattopadhyaya bitterly opposed the series of negotiations between the Congress leaders and the British government during the progress of the Civil Disobedience Movement. Indian leaders, who were not Congressmen but were trying to bring out a rapprochement between the nationalists and the imperialists such as Sir Tej Bahadur Sapru, M.M. Jayakar, and Srinivasa Sastri were dubbed as 'imperialist agent[s]'; he did not believe that Jawaharlal Nehru would oppose elder Congress leaders. But he was hopeful about the radical role of the masses. He concluded, '... but the tremendous danger of the revolutionary mass movement will compel both sides to find the form that is necessary to preserve imperialist interests on the one hand and be "inoffensive to national self-respect" on the other.'[55]

The denunciation of the moderates and Congressmen in Indian politics by Chattopadhyaya stemmed directly from his allegiance to Comintern's unconcealed hostility to the second Socialist International, termed by them as 'Social Fascist and Social Imperialist International ...'[56] Chattopadhyaya's article 'International Social Fascism supports MacDonald's Terrorism in India.' reflects his unwavering adherence to Comintern's position.

He calls MacDonald's Government 'as agents of British Fascism at home and Lackeys of British imperialism in the colonial countries.'[57] Commenting on the resolution passed by the Executive Committee meeting of the Socialist International at Zurich wherein India was specifically discussed, he noted,

That resolution contained *no word of condemnation* (emphasis added) for the methods by which the interests of British imperialism were being maintained in India by a member of the Second International. It was marked by suppression of the freedom of speech, of the press and of assembly, bribery and corruption, brutal prison torture, police and military terror, mass arrests, hanging and shootings, and government by machine guns, tanks, and bombing planes.[58]

He ridiculed the Labourite protestations because he pointed out,

Thirdly, the resolution definitely accepts the British Empire as compatible with fundamental principles of Socialism, for it urges the "Labour Government"—not to withdraw its army from India, not to abandon its repression and terror, not to recognise India's claim to independence, but—to grant India "self-government" i.e. self-government within the British Empire in accordance with the fundamental principles of Socialism and the Labour movement![59]

Chattopadhyaya was, however, not blind to the significance of the struggle being conducted by the Congress against British rule though at the same time he was conscious of the setback its success could cause to the Communist movement. His essay, 'Increased Revolutionary Activity in India'[60] clearly indicates his awareness of these trends. The arrest of the members of the Congress Working Committee at Delhi on 25 August 1930, including such moderate leaders as Dr. M.A. Ansari and Madan Mohan Malaviya, showed that the Government had been pressurised by British capitalists to control the movement.[61]

Chattopadhyaya conceded that the ongoing movement was fairly widespread and that in the two months ending June, 15, 989 persons had been arrested.[62] The politicisation of the masses as a consequence of the movement had its plus points from the Communist point of view. For example, in Lyalpur (now in the Punjab province of Pakistan) members of Naujawan Bharat Sabha appeared in red shirts before a court and raised the slogan, *'Mahatama Lenin Ki Jai.'* Chattopadhyaya concluded, 'There is not the least doubt that there will be a considerable intensification of the revolutionary movement during the next few months, accompanied, of course, by more severe repression than India has yet been subjected to under any other government in Great Britain.'[63]

Chattopadhyaya returned to the theme of the negotiation going on between the Congress and the British government in his article, 'The Breakdown of the "Peace" Negotiations in India.'[64] His assessment after examining the correspondence that had passed between the Congress leaders, Viceroy, and the liberal leaders such as Sapru and Jayakar, was that the "failure" be regarded as temporary'.[65] He was clear that 'industrial unemployment with its consequences, agrarian revolts, terrorism, failure of the boycott, diminishing trade, and other factors must soon compel the industrialists, merchants, landowners and professional classes [would put pressure], upon the Congress to "call off" their Movement.' Chattopadhaya believed that the Indian Natiional Congress could not lead the fight against imperialism and colonialism. He stuck to this view while commenting on the ensuing Round Table Conference which was to begin at London from 10 November 1930. He captioned this piece as 'The Indian Circus in London.'[66]

The Indian participants were described as '... some of 65 of the best trained Indian animals of various species ... chosen to perform in order to advertise the indispensability of British trainer that holds these mutually hostile animals back from devouring one another.'[67] He was very severe on Moulana Mohammad Ali,

> who had for years led the Muslims to fight for independence from British imperialism, and who as late as the Summer of 1928 sent a delegation to the International Secretariat of the League Against Imperialism in which he said that it was "the duty of every true Muslim to overthrow imperialism wherever it was found and whatever form it manifested itself." Today he asks the Muslims of Arabia to fight for independence and the Muslims of India to accept a compromise with British imperialism!.

It was a scathing criticism and a fine piece of satirical writing and a clear view of the role some Muslim leaders were playing in Indian politics.

Chattopadhyaya continued to criticise the Congress, the Civil Disobedience Movement, the policies of the Labour Government in Great Britain led by Ramsay MacDonald and the Round Table Conference. He felt that Congress was the main hurdle in the radicalisation of the masses in India. In his piece, 'The Indian National Congress Against Revolutionary Development,' he explicitly stated: 'But the real struggle that is going on is not between the Congress and British imperialism but between the Congress and the Indian revolutionary movement.' He went on to say, 'in fact the present policy of the Congress is to become a Kuomintang, with the object of establishing an Indian Nanking with the blood of the workers and peasants.'[68] Little wonder, fed on such a diet of anti-Congressism in the early 1930s, the Indian Communists failed to understand the significance of the Quit India Movement launched by Gandhi in 1942.

The last issue of *Inprecor* of the year 1930 carried an overall assessment of the work done at the Round Table Conference during the previous six weeks. Chattopadhyaya had no hesitation in saying,

> The 'enormous difficulties' of granting 'responsible self-government' to India are being deliberately illustrated by the conflict that has been taking place between the Muslims and Hindus at the Conference ... But the Hindu-Muslim question does not exist outside the ranks of the jobhunters. The workers and peasants are united in their economic and political demands, and so soon as they free themselves completely from the 'guidance' of their bourgeois and petty bourgeois leaders, the whole 'federal Union' of the imperialists and their agents will be annihilated and the true Federal Republic of the Workers and Peasants established.[69]

Little did Chattopadhyaya realise that the chasm between the Hindus and the Muslims was widening and not narrowing!

Chattopadhyaya was unable to appreciate the deep divide existing between the Hindu and Muslim politicians. He was carried away by the Marxist rhetoric so much that he glossed over the irreconcilable elements between the two communities.

VIII

Since the Round Table Conference was then the most hotly debated topic in Indian politics, Chattopadhyaya returned to it in an article entitled, 'MacDonald's New Imperialist Constitution for India.' (*Inprecor*, Vol. 11, No. 3, pp. 46-7). Its conclusion was in keeping with his earlier assessments. He wrote,

> imperialism has every reason to be satisfied for, ... it has evolved a scheme by which the cooperation of the Indian owning classes is assured both against the rising tide of Indian Revolution as well as against the Soviet Union and the rapidly emerging Soviet China.[70]

Then he went on to examine the provisions of the federal constitution, evolved after deliberation. For example,

Chattopadhyaya says, 'another power reserved to the Viceroy is the right of "protecting minorities", which is the British imperialist way of saying "the right to make minorities quarrel among themselves"'.[71]

The negative assessment of the Round Table Conference did not deter Chattopadhyaya from remaining an optimist. He felt,

> The agrarian crisis and the consequently revolutionary movement among the peasantry, as well as the rapid radicalisation of the Indian workers, are the factors that will force the Congress leaders to continue in India the negotiations begun in London.[72]

His faith in masses and an imminent revolution remained unshaken.

Chattopadhyaya's style shows that he carefully marshalled facts, then went to history to put them in proper context and finally, he drew conclusions couched in Marxist rhetoric.

His faith in the ability of the masses to set right every matter mismanaged by politicians remained unshaken; he continued to pour scorn over Congress, non-Marxist Indian leaders and the British government. The first issue of *Inprecor* of the year 1931 carried an article by Chattopadhyaya entitled MacDonald's New Year "Honours List for India." He pointed out that the awardees included eighty-two members of the Indian Police Force. His intention was to show that 'the New Year Honours List, it is true, is merely a list of imperialist agents, but our analysis has shown how even such a list may throw light on the workings of imperialist policy.'[74]

While he dealt with the Congress policies, Chattopadhyaya was also keen that his organization, League Against Imperialism, should have a full-fledged branch in India because [as he thought] it alone had the potential to lead masses to revolution. When the first All-India Anti-

Imperialist Conference was convened in Bombay on 24 October 1930 to establish an All-India Anti-Imperialist League, Chattopadhyaya thought fit to publish resolutions adopted by it along with a short note outlining the history of the League.[76]

The note recalled that the League was founded in Brussels in February 1927 when for the first time the Congress of Oppressed Peoples met. Jawaharlal Nehru who attended it as the representative of the Indian National Congress was elected a member of the International Executive of the League. It was expected that he would establish a branch of the League in India; but Nehru demurred on the plea that the Indian National Congress was 'the only comprehensive anti-imperialist organisation in India.'[77] Meanwhile, Chattopadhyaya pointed out that Congress leaders had started negotiating 'a compromise with British Imperialism; in this context the meeting of the Anti-Imperialist Conference at Bombay was an event of considerable significance.' Its importance was all the more greater as

> ... the rank and file of the Indian National Congress are likely to break away from the capitalist leadership, and that the revolutionary movement among the masses is rapidly growing, the Indian League is likely to play an important part in co-ordinating all the forces and giving a correct direction in the struggle for the overthrow of the British imperialism.[78]

Needless to say, Chattopadhyaya was over-optimistic; except for a handful of political activists, people hardly knew about this foreign organization. There was no outbreak of a rebellion; politics in India continued to chart its steady course.

Chattopadhyaya however, failed to understand the realities and intricacies of Indian political life. He persisted with his anti-Congressism, which was evident in the devastating denunciation of the Gandhi-lrwin Pact of March 1931 in a front page article entitled, 'The Capitulation of the Indian Bourgeoisie.'[79] He blasted Nehru for not being true to his declaration of January 1930 that the Congress was for a fight to the finish with British imperialism.[80] He described Gandhi as 'the political agent of the Indian landlords, money-lenders and the industrial and commercial bourgeoisie.'[81] His anger against Gandhi was evident in the following sentences:

> The theoretician of the Indian owning class, the man that gave to the greed and the cowardice of the Indian bourgeoisie the cloak of ethics and the instrument of the mass struggle was Gandhi. Himself a product of the causiries (*sic*) of Hindu religion and the hypocrisies of British constitutional law, he has been all throughout his life an admirer of the British Empire and an active supporter of British militarist aggression. Whether in his earlier career in South Africa or in the last ten years of his nefarious domination of Indian politics, the movements of resistance he has ever organised against the 'satanic government' of Great Britain have always been broken off at the point where they began to be dangerous to the property of the owning class or to the cooperation between these and British imperialism.[82]

Despite his vehemence, objectivity did not desert him. He conceded that Gandhi 'was the first bourgeois leader to understand the power of organised mass discontent, and he enunciated methods and solutions that suited the petty-bourgeois mentality and feudal-religious tradition that form the strongest supports of the propertied classes.'[83]

Chattopadhyaya then went on to delineate the twelve stages through which Gandhi passed before he struck a compromise with British imperialism. He did not spare Jawaharlal Nehru: 'Thus the radical phraseology of Nehru is just a manoeuvre intended to enable Gandhi to implement the betrayal.'[84]

IX

Despite his disenchantment with political leadership, Chattopadhyaya remained hopeful. On the leadership issue he commented: 'this final capitulation of the bourgeoisie is a positive gain to the working masses, for it emancipates them from the illusions created by the Congress leaders.' But he admitted,

> while there is no doubt that it is the proletariat that will henceforth, take up the full leadership of the struggle against imperialism, the working class itself is going through a struggle against the reformist and pseudo-communist element so that [they] are attempting to turn the workers away from a clear revolutionary class programme to treacherous class collaboration.

Chattopadhyaya's analysis may today seem extremely biased and utopian, but let us not forget that he was constrained to mouth communist clichés as laid down by the Comintern. However, his love for the country and passion for its independence had remained undiminished. He tried to enlist, through the medium of *Inprecor*, international support for its ongoing struggle against colonialism and imperialism.[85]

The *Inprecor* of 19 March 1931 carried an appeal by the International Secretariat of the League entitled, 'Long Live Independent India! Appeal of the League Against Imperialism. To the Indian people.' It sought to warn the masses against the policies of the top leaders of the Indian National Congress. The appeal stated,

> The League Against Imperialism is aware of the fact that the Indian National Congress has been an associate member of the League since 1927 and that Jawaharlal Nehru is still a member of the International Executive. But in view of the treacherous bargain that organisation and its President Nehru have entered into with imperialism, the next session of the International Executive will take the necessary actions to remove the Indian National Congress

from its list of associated organisations and to expel Jawaharlal Nehru from the Executive. We feel sure that in doing so the League will have the wholehearted support of the Indian masses.

The appeal concluded with slogans among which one read, 'Down with Gandhism which supports imperialist exploitation.'[86]

The Comintern was convinced of the failure of the Congress to bring about an armed uprising against the British rule. It, therefore, chose to vent its ire upon its leadership. On the same page *Inprecor* (19 March 1931) carried a statement issued by the Communist Party of Great Britain entitled, 'Against Imperialist Oppression in India.' It related to trial of Bhagat Singh and Batukeshwar Dutt, the two great Indian revolutionaries; it noted,

The history of this so called trial, unparalleled in the history of political persecution, is characterised by the most inhuman and brutal treatment which is the outcome of a frantic desire on the part of the Labour Imperialist Government to strike terror into the hearts of an oppressed people![87]

The most poignant part of this statement refers to Jatin Das who had died after a heroic hunger strike of 63 days in a British prison.

'Jatin Das had become paralysed, blind, and his blood circulation only operated in the near vicinity of his heart. He had in the process of hunger striking, been forcibly fed until such forcible feeding became a danger to his life. His body had been reduced by 60-lbs. in weight, and only weighed 19-lbs. at his death.'[88]

Chatto continued to vent his ire against Indian National Congress.

In another front-page article of *Inprecor* (1 August 1931) entitled, 'The Indian National Congress' he again reverted to the theme of betrayal of the Indian masses by the Congress.[89] He exhorted,

In order to free the masses finally from the national reformist leadership, it is necessary to carry on a wide campaign against the National Congress and in particular to expose the real role of Nehru, Bose and other leaders who still wield influence in working-class and peasant organisations.[90]

The anti-Congress obsession was evident in another article, 'Release the Meerut Prisoners!'[91] He espoused the cause of thirty-one prisoners languishing in gaol for being communists and supporters of the Soviet Union. He wrote,

The role of the Indian National Congress during the last two years in regard to the Meerut prisoners must be exposed. A 'Central Defence Committee' was established at Delhi, consisting of Nehru, Ansari and other prominent Congress leaders. The defence of the Meerut prisoners was used for some time as a lever against the Government, but hardly any money was collected for their defence and within a few months the Committee was liquidated.'

Going further he pointed out, 'but in the Pact with the British Government, Gandhi and his colleagues completely abandoned the Meerut prisoners.'[92]

He would not give up the cause of Meerut prisoners whom he rightly called Indian patriots, keenly devoted to the cause of Indian independence. He noted,

the urgent need of organising an international campaign on the broadest possible basis to denounce the imperialist brutality of the Labour Government; to expose the role of the British T.U.C. which supports the labour Government by refusing to give financial or any-other aid to the Indian working class leaders in Meerut Jail; to expose the tactics of the I. L. P. whose leading members withdraw from the National Meerut Defence Committee formed in London and who support Gandhi and other traitors of the Indian National Congress; ... and above all to exercise the strongest possible pressure on the MacDonald Government by setting up a strong international demand by the workers of Europe and America for the immediate release of the Meerut prisoners.[93]

Thus 1930 was the dividing line in the relationship between Congress and the Communist Parties. From the beginning of 1931 Comintern's attack on Congress leadership became shriller and Indian Communists followed the Comintern line in criticizing Indian National Congress.

For around two months Chattopadhyaya did not write anything in *Inprecor*. At this stage we have no idea why this happened. His primary concern by now appears to have undergone a subtle change; he was more concerned with promoting the Comintern ideology and exposing the lurking dangers to the existence of the Soviet Union. Probably, changes in the management of LAI [League Against Imperialism] forced him to keep mum. The secretariat of the LAI was moved to Paris. Nehru was expelled. The Communist control over the organization was a reality. It was now a representative of Comintern. (Baruah, p. 266)

He broke his silence in the issue of 18th June 1931 by a front-page essay entitled 'Strengthening Anti-Soviet Front in Near-East. Effects of New Press Decree in India.' It dealt with Lord lrwin's press policy. He stated, 'And thirdly, he introduced a completely new feature by giving protection to the foreign vassals of British Imperialism in the countries surrounding India.'[94] The Foreign Relations Ordinances laid down that any publication 'likely to promote unfriendly relations between His Majesty's Government and a foreign Government is liable to prosecution and confiscation.'[95] Under this Ordinance, the British Government started muzzling Indian Press when it published, for example, the Afghan King Amanullah's brochure criticising his brother, Afghan king Nadir Shah, an ally of the English.[96] Similarly, the British Government adopted punitive measures when a manifesto issued by rebels against Reza Shah Pehlevi (ruler of lran) was printed by Indian newspapers; the British swore friendship to Reza Khan.[97]

Chattopadhyaya brought into open the duplicity of British. He pointed out,

> But the word 'friendly government' does not apply to the Soviet Union, and no Indian journal is prosecuted for publishing the most infamous lies or using the most abusive language against the Soviet Union. The foreign Relations Ordinate is another measure in Britain's war preparations.[98]

The last paragraph clearly spelled Chattopadhyaya's preference: the journal was to safegurad the interests of the Soviet Union.

For the next twenty-one issues Chattopadhyaya did not publish anything. We do not know why this happened. When he published his next article it was a politically harmless piece entailed, 'Timber Export and Forced Labour in the Andaman Island.'[99] Along with the usual denunciation of imperialism was the desire to disprove the charge of the use 'forced labour' by the Soviet Union for producing goods being exported to Europe. He pointed out that the Andaman timber was collected chiefly cut by 'convict labour.'[100] Hence, he concluded, 'when, therefore, any imperialist opens his mouth about forced labour in the Soviet Union, the blood-soaked timber of the Andamans should be thrust down his hypocritical throat.'[101]

Again after a gap of nine issues, Chattopadhyaya wrote a piece, 'International Imperialism arms Afghanistan'.[102] It did not directly deal with the Indian political scene but was primarily concerned with the re-arming of Afghans by the British, German, Italian, French, Japanese, etc., The author's conclusion was, 'whatever may be the mutual antagonisms among the imperialists themselves, they are all united in their hatred of the Soviet Union and Soviet China.'[103]

Afghanistan had a long common border with the Asian republics of the Soviet Union and could serve as a launching pad for an invasion against the Bolshevik regime. Hence, Chattopadhyaya was keen that it remained neutral between the Soviets and the imperial powers.

It is a measure of Chattopadhya's versatility that he could write on political scenario of other colonies with equal ease. The issue no. 34 of vol. 10 carried three pieces by Chattopadhyaya (i) 'the Anti-Imperialist Movement in Egypt,' (ii) 'Iraq as Britain's Base Against the Soviet Union' and (iii) 'the First International Conference of Negro Workers.' [104]

X

Chattopadhyaya's other publication during this period include: 'The Indian Railway Strike' in *The Pan-Pacific Monthly* (April 1930), 'India and the Second International' in ibid., no. 37, (June-July 1930), 'The Indian Revolution and Natinalist Leaders' in ibid., and 'The Indian National Congress' in *The Labour Monthly*, 13(5), *May 1931* (Baruah, p. 385).

Chattopadhyaya wrote an article on Egypt entitled, 'British Imperialism and Egyptian Nationalism.'[105] In line with his Marxist ideology he dubbed Egyptian nationalists as 'representing the growing demands of native capitalism.'[106]

Shifting his gaze temporarily from the Round Table Conference, Chattopadhyaya published a well-informed piece on the peasant revolt that had broken out in the district of Tharawaddy in Burma.[107] He first described its history of resistance, its high literacy rate and the immediate circumstances, which prompted the peasantry to take up arms. His concluding lines are,

> ... millions of Burmesse peasants, although nominally owners of their holdings, have been completely expropriated by imperialist exploitation; moral indebtedness has grown to a hopeless figure,

unemployment is increasing among all sections of the toiling masses. There is no way out except an agrarian revolution which will destroy imperialism and its agents, ...[108]

Chattopadhyaya's comparative silence during the later half of 1931 was probably caused by developments taking place in Germany. The Socialists were on retreat and the Nazis were gradually becoming the dominant force in German political life. The racist Nazis hated communists and were increasingly targeting the League. In one of the attacks by Nazis, the office of the League was ransacked; the official documents were burnt and threat to life loomed large. Chattopadhyaya was advised to leave for Moscow to escape from the Nazi threats. He arrived in Moscow, and this brought an end to another adventurous chapter in his political career, the German years, which extended from 1914 to 1932 (barring the years spent in Stockholm).

As a co-secretary of the League with Muenzenberg, Chattopadhyaya rendered distinguished services to it by organising branches all over the world and by coordinating their activities. When he became associated with *Inprecor*, within an year and a half (January 1930 to June 1931) he regularly wrote in its pages on the problems facing the struggles being waged in the colonies and the imperial policies and stratagems to contain them; the villain of the game was always the 'bourgeoisie', 'the capital' and the Second International and Indian National Congress.

It must, however, be admitted that Chattopadhyaya never omitted facts: the evidence was carefully collected. Only in his conclusion, did he stick to the line laid down by the Comintern and remained loyal to the cause of the Soviet Union. However, despite his need to conform to the ideal of the League, Chattopadhyaya never forgot the freedom struggle going on in his motherland. He had left the country in 1900 and so was out of touch with the pulse of the people. Nevertheless, he tried to read whatever was published on

India in the foreign press and whatever other literature on India he could lay his hands upon.

In the 1920s, he tried to befriend Indian students, political leaders, and others who visited Berlin and tried to learn the mood of his countrymen, but this could never be as instructive as first hand knowledge. Circumstances denied Chattopadhyaya the chance to personally observe what was going on in India, and hence his comments and analysis failed to capture the mood of the Indians and the real contribution made by 'bourgeois leaders' such as Gandhi, Jawaharlal Nehru, and others like them. Even when he gave up pistol and took up pen, he continued to serve the Indian freedom struggle with sincerity and total selflessness.

Endnotes

1 Baruah, N.K. 2004. *Chatto The Life and Times of an Anti-Imperialist in Europe*, Delhi: Oxford University Press, pp. 252–3.
2 Surendra Gopal, 'An Island of Hope: Indian Patriots in Germany in 1920s', *History*, Vol. 2, No. 1, pp. 34–6.
3 ibid., p. 39.
4 *Inprecor*, 27 February, 1930.
5 *Inprecor*, Vol. 10 No. 14, 20 March 1930, p. 42.
6 *Inprecor*, 23 February, 1930 Vol. 10, No. 11, pp. 184–5.
7 ibid., Vol. 10, No. 12, p. 209.
8 ibid., p. 210.
9 *Inprecor*, Vol. 10, No. 21, 30 April 1930, pp. 381–2.
10 ibid., p. 382.
11 ibid., p. 382.
12 *Inprecor*, Vol. 10, No. 22, 8 May 1930, p. 399.
13 It would be interesting to know who this gentleman Sanyal was, *Inprecor*, Vol. 10, No. 24, 22 May 1930, p. 429.
14 ibid.
15 ibid., p. 430.
16 ibid.
17 ibid., p. 435.
18 ibid., p. 436.
19 ibid.
20 *Inprecor*, Vol. 10, No. 25, 28 May, 1930, p. 445.
21 ibid., p. 445–6.
22 ibid., p. 436.

23 *Inprecor,* Vol. 10, No. 27, p. 486.
24 ibid., p. 487.
25 ibid.
26 ibid., p. 489.
27 ibid.
28 ibid.
29 *Inprecor,* Vol. 10, No. 28, p. 503.
30 ibid.
31 ibid.
32 *Inprecor,* Vol. 10, No. 37, 14 August 1930, p. 737.
33 ibid., p. 738.
34 *Inprecor,* Vol. 10, No. 28, pp. 505–6.
35 *Inprecor,* Vol. 10, No. 29, p. 528.
36 ibid., p. 529.
37 *Inprecor,* Vol. 10, No. 30, p. 545.
38 *Inprecor,* Vol. 10, No. 31, p. 560.
39 ibid., p. 518.
40 *Inprecor,* Vol. 19, No. 29, 19 June 1930, p. 517.
41 ibid., p. 518.
42 *Inprecor,* Vol. 10, No. 29, p. 527.
43 *Inprecor,* Vol. 10, No. 30, p. 543.
44 ibid., p. 544.
45 ibid., pp. 544–5.
46 ibid., p. 545.
47 *Inprecor,* Vol. 10, No. 31, p. 559.
48 ibid., p. 560.
49 *Inprecor,* Vol. 10, No. 35, pp. 665–6.
50 *Inprecor,* Vol. 10, No. 41, 4 September 1930, pp. 858–9.
51 ibid., p. 859.
52 V. Chattopadhyaya, 'Six Weeks of the Indian Round Table Conference', *Inprecor,* Vol. 10, No. 60, 31 December 1930, p. 1243.
53 ibid., p. 746.
54 ibid., p. 746.
55 *Inprecor,* Vol. 10, No. 40, pp. 827–8.
56 ibid., p. 831.
57 ibid., p. 832.
58 ibid., p. 832.
59 ibid.
60 *Inprecor,* Vol. 10, No. 41, 4 September 1930, p. 853.
61. ibid.
62 ibid., p. 854.
63 ibid.
64 *Inprecor,* Vol. 10, No. 43, pp. 905–6.
65 ibid., p. 905.

66 *Inprecor*, Vol. 10, No. 45, pp. 952–3.
67 ibid., p. 952.
68 *Inprecor*, Vol. 10, No. 50, p. 1036.
69 V. Chattopadhyaya, 'Six Weeks of the Indian Round Table Conference', *Inprecor*, Vol. 10, No. 60, 31 December 1930, p. 1243.
70 ibid., p. 46.
71 ibid., p. 47.
72 ibid.
73 ibid.
74 *Inprecor*, Vol. 11, No. 1, 7 January, 1931, p. 5.
75 ibid.
76 *Inprecor*, Vol. 11, No. 4, pp. 79–80 and Vol. 11, No. 5, pp. 104–5.
77 *Inprecor*, Vol. 11, No. 4, p. 79.
78 ibid.
79 *Inprecor*, Vol. 11, No. 15, 19 March 1931, pp, 265–86.
80 ibid.
81 ibid.
82 ibid.
83 ibid., p. 286.
84 ibid.
85 ibid., pp. 294–5.
86 ibid., p. 295.
87 ibid., p. 295.
88 ibid.
89 *Inprecor*, Vol. 11, No. 19, 9 April 1931, pp. 361–3.
90 ibid., p. 363.
91 *Inprecor*, Vol. 11, No. 20, pp. 383–4.
92 ibid., p. 383.
93 ibid., p. 384.
94 *Inprecor*, Vol. 11, No. 32, 18 June 1931, p. 574.
95 ibid.
96 ibid.
97 ibid.
98 ibid.
99 *Inprecor*, Vol. 11, No. 54, pp. 985–6.
100 ibid.
101 ibid., p. 986.
102 *Inprecor*, Vol. 11, No. 62, pp. 1122–3.
103 ibid., p. 1123.
104 *Inprecor*, Vol. 10, No. 34, pp. 627–28 and pp. 635–6.
105 *Inprecor*, Vol. 10, No. 35, pp. 667–8.
106 ibid., p. 667.
107 V. Chattopadhyaya, 'The Peasant Revolt in Burma', *Inprecor*, Vol. 11, No. 2, pp. 37–8.
108 ibid., p. 38.

2

Engaging with B.R. Ambedkar's Construction of Hindu Society and Religion

L.S. Vishwanath

Introduction

It is evident to anyone who reads B. R. Ambedkar's writings on the Hindu caste system, Hinduism, and Buddhism that he not only addressed these subjects but also wrote extensively on them. Yet, except a few sociologists, most students of Indian society seem to have neglected his writings. This is surprising in view of the fact that Ambedkar's writings deal with issues which the scholars researching the caste system in India have been debating for quite sometime. For example, Ambedkar was firmly of the view that the Hindu religion, particularly the religious sanctity accorded in it to the Brahmin who, as he put it was a 'superman' accounted for and the basis of the hierarchy and inequality of the caste system. In a similar vein, Dumont stressed upon the ritual purity of the Brahmin and on general notions of purity in the Hindu religion to explain caste hierarchy. In his book, *Homo Hierarchicus*, Dumont argued that the basis of hierarchy in the Hindu caste system was the ideology of purity in Hindu religion which had, as its underlying principle, the opposition of the pure and impure which encompassed power. We must note the difference. While Ambedkar stressed that the 'soul' of caste inequality was the Hindu religion, Dumont brought in the dimension of power, that is, *artha* which is devalued in relation to its complement, *dharma*. Dumont's work provoked considerable discussion and debate on whether power derived from ownership of material resources or notions of purity drawn from the Hindu religion was the basis of caste hierarchy. Though Dumont admits that a good many anthropologists who responded to his work, had not accepted his thesis, he reiterates the need for a holistic framework to understand caste hierarchy. (Dumont, 1980). It seems to me that Dumont's arguments for a holistic understanding of caste as a hierarchical system in the framework of the Hindu religion has validity. Field studies have contributed to an understanding of caste at the local level in a village and perhaps the region where the village is located. But in a country like India, with its long history and tradition, the need for a holistic understanding of caste in relation to the Hindu religion can hardly be overstated.

Another aspect of the debate on the Hindu caste society is whether it is an open or a closed system of stratification. Though in his writings Ambedkar occasionally refers to the 'dynamics of caste and class,' there is no doubt that he viewed caste as an unchanging and closed system which oppressed the dalits. Most sociologists seem to agree that the caste system opened up during colonial rule. To get a better perspective on the caste system and social mobility, it is necessary to examine the social history of pre-colonial India. I will try to do this in the light of the available research findings. A third area of debate concerns the conquest of India by the Muslim invaders and later by the British. Ambedkar firmly holds that conquest of India was due to caste and the varna order which forbade the shudra from carrying arms. However, military historians think differently and point to the control of the horse trade and some other factors to which I shall refer in a later section of this paper.

Besides the issues noted above, the other topics which Ambedkar discussed in his writings include: the role of religion in society, Hindu philosophy, reform of Hindu society and Buddhism. Though Ambedkar's writings should have been of interest to the students of Indian society, why were they neglected for decades after independence? It could be that Ambedkar's tireless work for the upliftment of the dalits led scholars to believe that he was mainly a political leader. Though some of his writings were published posthumously, a good many of his writings on caste and Hinduism were available through publications before his death. Hence, the reason cannot be for want of published materials. Ambedkar's writings and speeches bring out how active he was throughout his life to serve the oppressed dalits. His representations before various committee, commissions and the round table conference bear ample testimony of the activist Ambedkar. But Ambedkar was also a serious student of India's economy and society. This side of his personality is reflected in his published writings on provincial finance in British India, the problem of the rupee, and on caste and religion in India.

As a highly educated dalit who was exposed to western liberal ideas, Ambedkar felt very keenly the incongruity between western values and what seemed to him to be a closed caste system where an individual's position in society was determined by his birth, occupation and lack of freedom to marry as per his choice owing to the endogamous rule. He expressed this incongruity forcefully in his writings by saying that the caste system had neither liberty nor equality nor fraternity. Yet, with all the mismatch between western liberal ideals and the inequality of caste, caste seems to have adapted in various ways to modernity.

In this paper, I propse to examine Ambedkar's ideas in the light of the research findings of modern sociologists and historians. I cannot claim that my reading is exhaustive;

perhaps it is adequate to engage with the ideas thrown up by Ambedkar's writings. Moreover, since I have been studying, for sometime, the social history of Colonial Gujarat, I have also tried to use my knowledge of that region.

Ambedkar on Religion and the Caste System in India

A perusal of Ambedkar's own writings suggest that he drew his conclusions on the Hindu religion and the caste system in India by comparing the socio-economic history of Europe and India, the writings of anthropologists on religion and caste, the ancient classical texts such as the Vedas, Shastras and the Upanishads, and his own bitter experiences of exclusion by upper caste Hindus. Even though he had, by dint of his own efforts, acquired the highest educational qualifications, it did not make a difference so far as caste prejudice was concerned.

Ambedkar argued that in the important area of socio-economic change, the historical experience of Europe and India were different. He tried to substantiate this argument by saying that it was 'the fallacy of the socialists' who assumed that just as in Europe, property or the material conditions of existence was source of power, the 'same is true of India or that the same was true of Europe in the past.' Ambedkar countered the materialist interpretation of history of the Marxists (for whom he then used the term socialists) by saying that 'religion, social status and property are all sources of power and authority ... One is predominant at one stage, the other is predominant at another stage'. (BAWS, Vol. 1: 45).

Ambedkar is taking a clear position here. In Hindu society, religion was the prime source of power. This is evident from his statement that among Hindus, the hierarchy of high and low 'dignities' which constitute the caste system was prescribed by the intellectual and priestly class of Brahmins whose authority to assign these different order of dignities was derived from the ancient classical texts such as the Vedas and the Shastras composed by the Brahmins.

While Ambedkar's perception of caste hierarchy as having a religious basis is no doubt important for an understanding of the Hindu caste system, it presents a certain difficulty. Before I point out that difficulty, it should be noted that in his speech before the Constituent Assembly in 1946 which was then debating the Panchayati Raj Bill, Ambedkar referred to the power of the touchable Hindus in a village to punish the untouchables if they dared to take out a procession or did not show the expected respect to the higher castes. (BAWS, Vol.5: 12–26). Though he does not refer, in that speech, to the landowners and others such as the touchable poor, power based on economic strength which is mainly the quantum of arable land owned in the village, is implied. How else could the powerful among the touchable castes exercise their authority over the hapless untouchables? It seems to me that such occasional and implied reference to the economic strength of the dominant among the touchable, does not resolve the difficulty which Ambedkar's perception of Hindu caste hierarchy presents.

A number of field village studies by sociologists and social anthropologists point to the power exercised by the dominant caste over non dominant touchable castes and, of course, the untouchable castes. In the village context, this power was based mainly on economic strength derived from landownership. (Srinivas, 1966: 14). The village studies also discuss the purity-pollution rules between higher and lower castes, particularly with reference to the exchange of food and they clearly indicate that these rules were an important aspect of caste hierarchy and inter-caste relations. (Mayer, 1960; Marriott, 1959: 92–107). The dominant caste and the village headman, who invariably belonged to the dominant caste, were rulers of the village. They were the upper caste in the village and had or had adopted through Sanskritisation the symbols of upper caste Hinduism. (Srinivas, 1966: 16–17). Economic strength based on land control and purity-pollution ideas derived from Brahmanic Hinduism existed and were expressed through caste hierarchy. It is an oversimplification to reduce the village caste hierarchy to relations of power. It is also contrary to social reality to say that the Hindu religion had overwhelming importance so far as caste hierarchy is concerned. The difficulty with Ambedkar is that drawing his inferences from the varna model, he goes overboard to stress the low position of the shudra and the religious aspect of caste hierarchy. While it is true that the poor among touchable Hindus practised untouchability, the powerful touchables who belonged to the dominant caste oppressed the dalits. There is also the fact that the dominant castes in most villages in rural India did not belong to the three higher varnas of the normative Sanskrit texts. That is, they were neither Brahmins, nor Kshatriyas nor even the trading community of Banias because, except for a token presence in the village, most Banias lived in towns which were centres of trade and commerce. Ambedkar admitted in at least two of his writings that 80 per cent of India's population were Shudras. (BAWS,Vol.7: 9–18). If the dominant castes in upwards of two thirds of rural India were Shudras and did not belong to the three higher varnas whatever their claims to the contrary may have been, then there is a problem in placing too much reliance on the normative texts to draw conclusions on caste hierarchy because, according to the normative texts, power and privilege lie with the three higher varnas and not with the Shudra varna. However, Ambedkar relies heavily for his understanding of the Hindu caste hierarchy on the normative texts.

In general, Ambedkar assigned a very important role to religion in society. He pointed out that religion is a 'live wire' and belief in the supernatural was only one aspect of religion.

His conception of a civil society was one where religion was a moralizing force. He stressed the importance of religion in social control and firmly believed that the foundation of any society should be a moral order. He went further and, like Durkheim, maintained that religion should give a sense of belonging to its members. (BAWS,Vol.5: 403–21). According to Ambedkar, Hinduism, with its caste system based on exclusions from top to bottom of the hierarchy, could not contribute to that feeling of belonging or sense of solidarity. (Ibid). Given the importance which he attached to religion in social life and his dissatisfaction with Hinduism, he looked for an alterative religion to which he could convert with his followers. He felt that Christianity, Islam and Sikhism were not suitable for conversion as they had the caste system. Eventually he converted to Buddhism with lakhs of his followers (almost all of them Mahars) in 1956. The ways in which Ambedkar interpreted the Buddha's message will be discussed later. How did Ambedkar interpret varna and caste and how did he perceive what he called the 'pyramid' of castes?

In his analysis of caste and varna, he took note of what the Bhagvad Gita and the Arya Samajists said, namely that the Chaturvarna order is not a hierarchy based on one's birth but one's innate qualities. He argued that actually this was not so. He said:

> While caste has completely perverted the Varna system it has borrowed the class system from the Varna system. *Indeed the class-caste system follows closely the class cleavages of the Varna system.* Looking at the caste system from this point of view one comes across several lines of class cleavage which run through this pyramid of castes dividing the pyramid into blocks of castes. The first line of cleavage follows the line of division noticeable in the ancient Chaturvarna system. The old system of Chaturvarna made a distinction between the first three Varnas the Brahmins, Kshatriyas, Vaishyas and the fourth Varna, namely the Shudra. The three former were classed as the regenerate classes. The

Shudra was held as the unregenerate class. This distinction was based upon the fact that the former were entitled to wear the sacred thread and study the Vedas. The Shudra was entitled to neither and that is why he was regarded as the unregenerate class. *The line of cleavage is still in existence and forms the basis of the present day class division separating the castes which have grown out of the vast class of Shudras from those which have grown out of three classes of Brahmins, the Kshatriyas and Vaishyas. This line of class cleavage is the one which is expressed by the terms High Castes and Low Castes and which are short forms for the High Class Castes and Low Class Castes.* (Italics mine-BAWS, Vol.3: 142–8).

In connection with the above statement of Ambedkar one may ask who the high and low castes in rural India were. Let us examine the position of the Shudras whom Ambedkar calls the 'unregenerate class' in Ambedkar's own state, Maharashtra.

In pre-colonial Maharashtra, there was an alliance at the political level between the dominant caste of Marathas and the Brahmins. The Brahmins regarded the Marathas as Shudras but then they reluctantly conceded Kshatriya status to the Marathas after Shivaji captured power. After his coronation with the help of a Brahmin, Shivaji proclaimed himself Chhatarapati. Though the Brahmin Peshwas usurped power, made Poona their capital, and reduced Shivaji's descendants to figurehead status, this did not significantly affect the alliance. Maratha sardars captured territory and emerged as princes in Baroda (the Gaikwads), Gwalior (the Scindias), and Indore (the Holkars). Throughout the period of Maratha rule, in most parts of Maharashtra, there was power sharing between the Brahmins and the Marathas in that the important offices were shared at pargana, taluk and village levels. In revenue collection, the pargana head was generally a Maratha and the Deshpande always a Brahmin. In the village, the headman was from the dominant caste of Marathas while the accountant, Kulkarni, was a Brahmin. (Fukazawa, 1998: 83).

The onset of British rule in western India upset the alliance of Brahmin and Maratha. The Brahmins withdrew the recognition of Kshatriya status to the Marathas and called them Shudras. Worse still from the viewpoint of the Marathas was the fact that the Brahmins availed of the educational opportunities offered by colonial rule and captured most of the jobs in government service. Though the British made changes in the revenue administration, the power of the dominant Maratha caste was not greatly eroded. The headman remained a key figure in village administration and its affairs. Besides the dominant Maratha caste and the peasant caste allied to them, known as the Kanbis, most villages in Maharashtra had dependent castes such as barbers, washermen, ironsmiths, weavers, carpenters, and the untouchable castes. In the village caste hierarchy, the dominant Marathas were the high castes and the servicing dependent castes were lower. However, in the eyes of the Brahmins who as Ambedkar rightly said arrogated to themselves the right to legitimize or not legitimize the order of dignities, the dominant caste of Marathas and the dependent castes were Shudras. The Marathas reacted to this 'insult' by joining Phule's anti-Brahmin organization, the Satya Shodak Samaj (founded 1875) and eventually dominated that body. (O'Hanlon, 1985; Jaffrelot, 2000).

Two questions arise in regard to Ambedkar's formulation of high and low castes. First, why did he repeatedly claim that the Shudras are low and powerless when sections of peasants actually enjoyed high status at the local level, exercised considerable clout as the dominant caste in their own state and in most parts of rural India and oppressed the dalits? To say that the Shudra was the position assigned to them by the Brahmins during colonial rule and they actually belonged to a higher varna as they in fact claimed, leaves us with a scenario of competing claims and does not solve the problem relating to the varna affiliation of the dominant caste. Second, Ambedkar published in 1946 a book titled: *Who were the Shudras? How they came to be the Fourth Varna in the Indo-Aryan Society*. Even if we leave aside for a moment the debate on whether there was in fact an Aryan invasion or immigration from outside the sub-continent, what Ambedkar said in that book is of relevance here. He said that the Shudras have 'largely been instrumental in sustaining the infamous system of Chaturvarna though it has been the primary cause of their degradation.' (BAWS, Vol. 7: 9–18).

It is interesting to note that before Srinivas first put forward in 1952 the concept of Sanskritisation in his Coorg book which became popular to understand social mobility and change, Ambedkar was talking of Shudras as those who were 'instrumental in sustaining Chaturvarna.' Ambedkar also stated in the same book that the Shudras of his day were actually Kshatriyas who had become degraded because long ago they had a fight with the Brahmins who refused to perform the sacred thread ceremony for them. (BAWS, Vol. 7). Now why is Ambedkar, who denounced Hinduism as a religion based on inequality due to its caste system and called the Chaturvarna system as 'infamous', giving the Shudras a higher varna status within Hinduism? The answer could be, as Zelliot has pointed out, that Ambedkar had an ambivalent relationship towards Hinduism. (Zelliot, 1998). In fact, Ambedkar tried to Sanskritise but gave it up as not worth the effort as the barrier of untouchability seemed insurmountable. The 1931 census which was the last census to collect the population statistics on the basis of caste, classified the population in Maharashtra according to varna. It showed that 3.9 per cent were Brahmins; the Kshatriyas accounted for 1.69 per cent and the Vaishyas were one per cent. The Shudra category 'dominated by the Maratha-Kanbis, a group of allied castes together totaled 31.19 per cent of the province. No other Jati of this varna reached upto 5 per cent of the population of Maharashtra. (Jaffrelot, 2000).

In case it is argued that I have given the example of only one province to engage with Ambedkar's ideas on caste hierarchy, one more instance may be given of pre-colonial and colonial south India.

In pre-colonial south India, the Chola and later the Vijayanagara kingdoms had an alliance similar to that in Maharashtra between the Brahmin and the local dominant caste. (Stein, 1980: 51). There was, however, a difference. While in pre-colonial Maharashtra, the Marathas sought Kshatriya status, the dominant non Brahmin castes in south India generally did not claim Kshatriya or Vaishya status. Sociologists and historians are in agreement that in pre-colonial and colonial south India, there were only two categories in terms of varna, that is, Brahmin and non Brahmin. The two intermediate varnas, Kshatriya and Vaishya, did not exist. (Dumont, 1980; Stein, 1980: 51; 212–13). In the agrarian system of the Cholas, the predominant landowners in the Nadu were non-Brahmins known as the Natars. In Vijayanagara, the non-Brahmin landowners were Naikars who were also chiefs. The point is that in the pre-colonial Hindu Kingdoms in south India, such as Chola and Vijayanagara, political and economic power was in the hands of those who, at that point in time, accepted non-Brahmin status as the works of historians suggest. In fact, the dominant non-Brahmin peasant castes in south India donated land to the Brahmins which were known as Brahmadeyas. The donation of land was done in an individual capacity or through the non-Brahmin assembly known as the Ur. (Karashima, 2001: 5–6).

Colonial rule in south India withnessed a keen rivalry between the Brahmins and non-Brahmins and, of course, resentment of the fact that the Brahmins relegated the non-Brahmins to Shudra status. This, and the Brahmin domination in government services, culminated in the anti-Brahmin movement. It is interesting to note that just as Ambedkar tried to project the Shudra as a powerless and deprived category who, though touchable, had low caste status, the leaders of the non-Brahmin movement claimed that after the takeover of south India by the Aryan Brahmins, the non-Brahmins had been rendered powerless. (1). However, a voting list prepared by the government of Madras Presidency in connection with the franchise reforms of 1919 showed that the non-Brahmins were the pre-dominant landowners in rural areas and formed the bulk of the property owners in urban areas. It showed that out of 2,37,036 wealthiest rural inhabitants paying land revenue of more than Rs. 30, just 15.27 per cent were Brahmins; out of 53,647 wealthiest urban inhabitants paying municipal tax of Rs. 5, only 20.38 per cent were Brahmins. (Washbrook, 1989: 212).

Hierarchy and Caste Mobility

The normative sanskrit texts where the position of the four varnas is fixed for all time, seems to have led Ambedkar to believe that the caste hierarchy is unchanging. This could be true of the untouchables known as Avarnas, most of whom were at the bottom of the socio-economic ladder; but it does not hold for the vast mass of peasants who tried to avail every opportunity to claim higher varna status. Throughout Indian history there was this dynamics of caste and class to which Ambedkar briefly refers but does not develop the point in his writings. In regard to caste mobility and the concept of Sanskritisation put forward by Srinivas, Dumont raised the point about actual acceptance of higher varna status. The situation on actual acceptance of the claim from lower to higher varna varied from one region to another and it is difficult to generalize. For example in the two regions we examined earlier, the Marathas were granted

Kshatriya status during pre-colonial rule but, as we have seen, this recognition was withdrawn during colonial rule. In south India, at least so far the Tamil country is concerned, the dominant peasants neither claimed nor were they granted Kshatriya status. The work of the historians of the Tamil region, based on inscriptional and other evidences, suggests that the temples which were centres of Brahminical Hinduism came to occupy an important place in socio-economic life during Chola and Pallava rule. (Stein, 1980; Champakalakshmi, 1996). Due to the overarching role of these centres of Brahmanical Hinduism, the peasants perhaps accepted non-Brahmin status. If this argument has any validity, then at that point in historical time, namely Chola and Pallava periods, the limits to claims to a higher *dvija* or twice born varna status by the peasant castes in parts of south India were set by the important role of the Brahmanical temples. That Brahmanical Hinduism did not always have a predominant role in south India is evident from the contest between Jainism and Hinduism in parts of the Tamil region. History records that the Pallava king, Mahendravarman (early 7th century, A.D.), converted to Jainsim but re-converted and became a Shaivaite. (Meenakshi, 1996: 121). Shravanbelgola in present day Karnataka seems to have been an important centre of Jainism in pre-colonial south India. We should remember here that the style of life and religion of the politically powerful was important in that the commoners who were not economically or politically dominant tended to follow the example of the higher ups. In Punjab for example, there was, due to centuries of Muslim rule, the influence of Islam on different Hindu communities including the Brahmins who learnt Persian. (Rao, 1977). An important aim of Dayanand Saraswati's Arya Samaj movement was to revive Vedic Hinduism in Punjab. Again in Punjab for similar reasons, namely centuries of Islamic influence, the overwhelming role of the Brahmins as the assigner of caste dignity so greatly emphasized by Ambedkar was at best marginal.

Ambedkar's perception of caste as a fixed hierarchical system is also borne out by his observation that: 'in the matter of status of a person, it is fixed and is hereditary. It is fixed because a person's status is fixed by the status of the caste to which he belongs ... a Hindu cannot change his status because he cannot change his caste". (BAWS, Vol.3: 142–48).

As Ambedkar said, it is true that caste cannot be changed. But evidence for pre-colonial India suggests that status change within caste was possible. Indeed a change from highway robbers to king and princes was possible. Take, for example, the Jats of the Agra-Mathura region in the eighteenth century. They were highway robbers and laid siege to Mughal caravans carrying goods from Agra to Surat which was an important port and centre of trade in those days. The Mughal empire was in decline and the weak kings who sat on the Delhi throne enlisted the support of the Jat chiefs in their factional fights. Support to a ruling king and his faction won for the Jats **jagirs** from which kingdoms were carved out. Bharatpur in Rajasthan was one such kingdom. (Singh, 1981: 114). Besides receiving jagirs, the Jat chiefs also conquered territory in parts of north India. This was possible in the uncertain conditions of the eighteenth century. The Jat kingdoms of Patiala, Nabha, Jind and Kythal emerged either from conquest or assignment of jagirs.

An Ahir kingdom emerged during the eighteenth century under similar circumstances. The Ahir chiefs extended support to the ruling faction in the Delhi court and were granted a **jagir** in the area around Rewari in present day Haryana. (Rao, 1977: 77–89). These kingdoms became princely states under colonial rule. In the instances cited, matters did not end with change in status from robber or ordinary chief to king of a territory; the Jat and Ahir chiefs, by fulfilling their ambition, set an example and mediated their style of life to their fellow caste men and others lower down the hierarchy. In several parts of north India, the Jats were and still are the dominant caste. This resulted in, if we may use the term, Jatization or Ahirization of the local culture. Thus different from Ambedkar's formulation of the Brahmin as the pre-dominant person who was a superman or **bhudevata** (god on earth) and mattered most among Hindus, we have the Jats and Ahirs setting the tone of social life in the regions where they dominated. (Srinivas, 2002).

What ended with the emergence of the British as the paramount power in the sub-continent was that efforts for upward mobility of castes through conquest of territory was stopped. However, the military history of India shows that during the early phase of their rule, the British formed army regiments and assigned sizeable amounts of land to peasants who supplied horses for their cavalry and joined the regiment. Thus, James Skinner, an Anglo-Indian by birth, played an important role in British conquest of north India by building up his cavalry regiment through recruitment of Jats, Ahirs, and Gujars who supplied horses and were rewarded with assignment of land which was liable to nominal revenue. (Alavi, 2001: 291). We must note that this status change within caste was not insignificant because sizeable land was acquired in return for military service. As Alavi notes 'Skinner clearly manipulated the aspirations of his troopers who measured **izzat** and martial status against that held by their predecessors in earlier polities, and in particular the Mughal Empire' (Ibid). The fact that the Mughal rulers, too, assigned land to those who contributed troops and cavalry and participated in their wars suggests that, though things were not exactly similar during Mughal and British rule, there was continuity as well as status change.

That the onset of colonial rule witnessed efforts of castes to claim a higher, twice born varna status when the British instituted the ten year census enumerations in the last quarter of the nineteenth century, and the fact that the opening of educational institutions led to a 'race' for education and jobs to avail of upward mobility by numerous castes (Srinivas, 1966) are perhaps well known and may not require detailed comment. Another avenue for mobility in the caste system was getting their own Purana written by ambitious castes which laid claim to higher varna status. (Das, 1968).

While there is, on the whole, consensus on providing opportunities through reservations for mobility of the scheduled castes and scheduled tribes since they suffered from all kinds of deprivations for centuries, reservations for backward classes (other than SCs and STs) seem to have been a contentious issue even in the 1930's as Ambedkar's writings show. He refers to 'the struggle between the backward classes and the untouchables.' The 'struggle' was related to the demand of the backward classes in the 1930's that they should be included among the depressed classes since they too were educationally and economically backward. This demand was in the context of the constitutional reforms of 1935. The untouchables, as Ambedkar notes, were opposed to the demand because, as he put it, the backward classes were 'not really untouchables' and, more importantly, their inclusion 'would have swelled to enormous proportions' the total number of depressed classes. What Ambedkar said in regard to the demand of the backward classes may have relevance for the current debate on the reservations for the other backward classes in institutions of higher education. He said:

> The proper course for these backward communities was to have asked to make a division of Touchable Hindus into advanced and backward and to have claimed separate representation for the Backward. In that effort the Untouchables would have supported them. But they did not agree to this and persisted in being included

among the depressed classes largely because they thought that this was the easier way of securing their object. (BAWS, Vol.5: 229–76).

In a research paper which he presented at an anthropology seminar at Colombia University in 1916, Ambedkar says that whatever 'open door character caste as class may have had in the past, it was "lost" and classes became "self enclosed units called castes."' The main reason for this, according to Ambedkar, is the endogamous rule. He further says that the emergence of hierarchy in the caste system was due to endogamy because the Brahmins 'closed the door' and refused to intermarry with those below them. Those lower down the social order followed suit and 'closed door' on those below them in imitation of the Brahmins and became endogamous units. Thus, with each level 'closing the door' by becoming endogamous, caste hierarchy emerged. (BAWS, Vol. 1: 5–22).

We should remember that in 1916, when Ambedkar presented his seminar paper on 'castes in India,' theories of origin were popular. In most of his later writings, Ambedkar maintained that along with the hierarchy of caste, 'endogamy is the most fundamental idea on which the whole fabric of caste is built'. (BAWS, Vol. 3: 142–8). It is difficult to say anything about theories of origin except that they were dismissed as 'conjectural history' (Radcliffe-Brown, 1952) with the emergence of structural anthropology in England. Viewed vertically, the caste hierarchy did comprise, as Ambedkar said, a number of endogamous units one below the other, though dispute on caste ranking at the middle levels of the hierarchy was not uncommon. However, viewed horizontally and in conjunction with the hypergamous norm, the boundaries of caste at the lower levels of the hierarchy were porous in many cases, and endogamy which Ambedkar considered as a 'most fundamental idea' of caste was abandoned. Thus, among large castes like the Jats, Ahirs, Gujars, Rajputs and the Patels of Gujarat, the upward movement of women due to the hypergamous rule, resulted in shortage of marriageable girls at the lower levels of the hypergamous hierarchy; this shortage of women forced the men in these castes to break the endogamous rule and marry tribal women or women from lower castes in the region. For the tribal women, such marriages meant integration into the caste system. For lower caste women (for example, Koli women in Gujarat) such marriages signified upward mobility. (Vishwanath, 2000: 161). Marriage by purchase known as **mol lana** unions and marriage through elopement known as **bhaga lana** unions were fairly common among the Jats. (Pradhan, 1975:84). Since the Jats, Patels and Rajputs have been practicing female infanticide (now foeticide) for generations (Vishwanath, 2004), the adverse female sex ratios made it difficult for these castes to maintain the endogamous rule. There are already reports of the Jats procuring women from Assam for marriage. The records for the colonial period talk of established brokers who provided wives to castes who needed them for a fee. (SRG, NWP, 1879, Vol. 5: 14–15). Since this transaction through middlemen of procuring women from outside the caste was done surreptitiously and the girl passed off as a Jatnee or Rajputnee in her conjugal village, it is difficult to estimate or quantify the violation of the endogamous rule. At any rate, it is clear that the endogamous rule was not rigidly followed among quite a few castes and much depended on situation and circumstance.

Since the non-Brahmin movements in south and west India denounced Brahmin dominance, Brahmanical ritual and the inequality of caste, Ambedkar no doubt perceived them as natural allies of his own movement for uplift of the dalits. He attended the non-Brahmin conference chaired by Shivaji's descendant, the Maharaja Shahu of Kolhapur, who claimed Kshatriya status and was angered when Brahmins accorded Shudra status to him. (Omvedt, 2004: 24). Shahu funded Ambedkar's second visit abroad for higher studies. Periyar, the prominent non-Brahmin leader from south India, visited Bombay in January, 1940 and met Ambedkar (ibid: 88). There is also the fact that Ambedkar dedicated his book, *Who were the Shudras*, to Phule, the leader of the non-Brahmin movement in Maharashtra. However, it is clear that Ambedkar was uneasy with the non-Brahmin interest and was not sure if they could represent the dalit interest. This uneasiness arose not only from the fact that they were touchables and did not suffer from the disabilities of the untouchables; Ambedkar had to reckon with the fact that the group which acquired a non-Brahmin identity in conditions of colonial rule was a highly diverse and heterogeneous category ranging from the very poor washermen, barber and weaver to the well-to-do landowning dominant castes. Not surprisingly, therefore, Ambedkar speaks of 'the struggle between the Untouchables and the backward classes' and to Shudras as the 'upholders of Chaturvarna' as noted above.

Reform of Hindu Society

To say that ridding Hindu society of the inequitable caste system was an important part of Ambedkar's plan of reforming Hindu society, is saying the obvious. At times he despaired of reforming Hindu society and said that instead of trying to reform a social order which seemed incapable of reform, it was better to opt out of Hinduism and convert to some other religion. Given that he belonged to a community which was, as he put it, 'outside the fold' or 'beyond the pale,' no major opportunity to reform Hindu society beyond representations before committees and commissions came his way till he was appointed Chairman of the drafting committee to draft India's Constitution and later when Nehru appointed him Law Minister in his

Cabinet. That Ambedkar played a key role as the Chairman of the drafting committee is evident from the provisions in the constitution such as reservations for the scheduled castes and tribes and abolition of untouchability.

Ambedkar chaired the drafting committee for the Hindu Code Bill which he later piloted in the lower house of Parliament. Before independence, in 1941, a committee headed by B.N. Rau had drafted a Bill for reforming Hindu law. But then the events leading to independence and the trauma of partition intervened. Many of the provisions in Rau's draft Bill, as also Ambedkar's, related to women's rights. Ambedkar's Bill gave daughter(s) in the Hindu family equal right with son(s) in intestate property. Further, as in the Hindu Women's Right to Property Act of 1937, the bill gave the widow and widow of a pre-deceased son a share in the father's property. In regard to marriage, Hindu women were better off under the provisions of the Bill drafted by Ambedkar because monogmy was prescribed while the old law permitted polygamy. Under the old law, Hindu marriage was indissoluble. Ambedkar's Bill contained provisions for the dissolution of the marriage subject to the conditions laid down in the Bill. (BAWS, Vol. 14, Pt. 1: 5–12). Nehru could not muster enough support to get the Hindu Code Bill passed and Ambedkar resigned from the Nehru Cabinet. In his resignation letter Ambedkar said that inequality of class (caste) and the sexes was the 'soul of Hindu Society' and to go on passing legislation which addressed only economic issues and not social ones was no better than 'to build a palace on a dung heap.' (BAWS, Vol. 14: 1325). There were other reasons for Ambedkar's resignation such as his disappointment at not being given the planning portfolio, the government policy on China and Kashmir and so on. (Jeffrelot, 2000; Omvedt, 2004).

In the long history of Hindu social reform, Ambedkar was, in modern times, the first dalit who wrote extensively on reform and played a key role in the first cabinet of free India. He often said that Hinduism had no future unless it reformed. To view the social reform project of Hindu society in perspective it is necessary to look at Ambedkar's efforts in the context of the efforts of other social reformers. First the efforts to eradicate untouchability.

The backward class leader, Mahatma Phule worked for improvement of the condition of untouchables. Phule started a school in Poona for untouchable girls and ran it in the teeth of opposition from upper castes. (O'Hanlon, 1985: 112). Among upper caste leaders who said that untouchability is not sanctioned by Vedic Hinduism and therefore should not be practiced was Swami Dayanand Saraswati. But, as Ambedkar pointed out, Dayanand and his Arya Samaj interpreted the Vedas to mean that the ancient Chaturvarna system was not a hierarchy based on birth but based on innate qualities. Ambedkar thought that such interpretations were merely at the level of interpretation; they did little to mitigate the harshness of the Hindu hierarchical caste system.

While other Hindu upper caste leaders had spoken against the practice of untouchability but never actively associated with the untouchables, the first Hindu upper caste leader who lived in untouchable bastis, dined with them, admitted an untouchable to his Ashram in Ahmedabad and made it a condition that he would attend weddings only if the bride belonged to the untouchable community, was Gandhi. (Parekh, 1986). Gandhi's lifelong campaign for eradication of untouchability focused the nation's attention on the inhuman and unjust practice because the Mahatma was widely respected for his moral authority, was an all-India figure, and the undisputed leader of the Congress which was fighting for the country's freedom from colonial rule. In the differences which Ambedkar had with Gandhi, the strategy for mitigating the problem of untouchability and solving it figured very prominently and was a core issue. Let us examine the position of each.

Gandhi took the position that the Hindu scriptures did not sanction untouchability and whatever evidence there was in the sacred texts was an interpolation. When this line of argument did not work with the orthodox Hindus known as Sanatanists, Gandhi adopted the strategy of arguing that the practice of untouchability was against the spirit of Hinduism which was a religion based on tolerance and further that the practice was indefensible on moral grounds. (Ibid). Gandhi's campaign against untouchability included fasts to stir the conscience of upper caste Hindus, insistence on the right of untouchability to enter Hindu temples and improvement programme. Gandhi's constructive programmes for the improvement of the untouchables covered, education, cleanliness, and prohibition of liquor. (Ibid: 228–65). Ambedkar for his part accused Gandhi of hypocrisy. He felt that given the bastions of Hindu orthodoxy, Gandhi's constructive programmes will not make even a dent in the problem of untouchability because they did not address the civic disabilities of the untouchables. Since he was a member of the Anti-Untouchability League constituted by Gandhi after the Poona pact of 1932, Ambedkar sent a comprehensive letter to A.V. Thakkar, the Secretary of the League in November, 1932 wherein he insisted that the League should work for specific civic rights of the untouchables such as the right to drinking water, access to roads, employment opportunities, and education. (BAWS, Vol. 9: 133–42). However, Ambedkar received no reply. Consequently, Ambedkar and two other untouchables resigned from the League. Thereafter, Gandhi renamed the League as the Harijan Sevak Sangh and took the decision to exclude untouchables from its membership. Despite the change in nomenclature, the Sangh's activities remained confined to the Gandhian constructive programme.

Though Gandhi took the line that since Caste Hindus were the ones who constributed funds for the organization and so they alone should have a say in its affairs, the real underlying reasons for not responding to Ambedkar's letter and the exclusion of the untouchable members seem to be different. As Parekh has pointed out, Gandhi worried about the militant postures of the untouchable leaders and did not wish to provoke a clash between the untouchables and Caste Hindus by insisting on civic rights of the former which could divide the Hindu camp and jeopardize the 'delicately balanced' freedom struggle. (Parekh, 1989: 270). Gandhi's objection to separate electorates for the untouchables was based on almost similar grounds. In the 1920s, Ambedkar went along with the demand that untouchables be allowed to enter Hindu temples. Later he attached more importance to rights such as access to drinking water, roads, representation in civic bodies and legislatures.

It is interesting to note that Gandhi and Ambedkar were aware of the social, economic, and political power structures of Indian society. Both worried about the shape of things to come once the British transferred power to Indian hands. Ambedkar worried that after the transfer of power to what he perceived as the upper caste dominated Congress, oppression of the untouchables might become worse. Gandhi was worried that the transfer of power may not usher in the egalitarian social order of his dreams. In **Hind Swaraj** he wrote:

> (You) want English rule without the Englishmen. You want the tiger's nature without the tiger, that is to say you would make India English. And when it becomes English, it will be called not Hindustan but Englishtan. This is not the Swaraj I want.

There is no doubt that if the cruel and unjust practice of untouchability still persists fifty five years after attainment of Swaraj, it is precisely due to the socio-economic power structures in Hindu society which are closely intermeshed with Hindu religion. Though Ambedkar said that there could be no true democracy unless the existing structures of power and authority were radically altered, he often said that the surest way to destroy the caste system was to put dynamite to the Shastras and other Hindu scriptures. (BAWS, Vol.1: 47–80). This is strange in view of his awareness of the power structures which were either religious or used religion to legitimize upper caste status. In fact, Ambedkar and his followers did burn a copy of the Manu Smriti at Mahad in Maharashtra in December 1927. (Gore, 1993; 106). It was perhaps a symbolic act. The results, as expected, were insignificant.

Ambedkar's efforts to push through the Hindu Code Bill which sought to give rights to Hindu women was not new when viewed in the context of the efforts of Hindu social reformers (mostly from upper castes) to rid Hindu society of Sati, to enable Hindu widows to re-marry, and to raise the age of marriage of Hindu girls. As noted in the literature on social reform, the nineteenth century Hindu social reformers were educated and were sensitive to the criticisms of their society by the Christian missionaries, the liberals, and the Utilitarians. Besides the iniquitous caste system, the low position assigned by Hindu society to its women was attacked. (Bandyopadhyay, 2004). Since the colonial government perceived Hindu society in terms of Hindu religion and scriptures and actually used the Shastras as Hindu law to adjudicate civil disputes, the reformers cited the Shastras to get the needed legislation passed. Citing the Shastras was also a strategy to counter the orthodox Hindus. Thus Ram Mohun Roy cited Manu Smriti to get Sati banned in 1928 and Vidyasagar cited Parashara Samhita to get a law passed in 1856 enabling Hindu widows to re-marry. (Mani, 1998; Sen,1977). Ambedkar also cited the Shastras while intervening in the debate on the Hindu Code Bill.

While the need to cite the Shastras for the social reform project seems obvious given the reasons noted above, it was not easy to reconcile the post-enlightenment western egalitarianism and individualism with Hindu patriarchy which gave women a subordinate position and also the fact that Hindu society generally upheld the ideals of family and community life. Reformers like Ram Mohun Roy and Swami Vivekananda spoke of a synthesis of what is best in modern western civilization and India's civilization without clearly spelling out how this was to be brought about. The fact is that the post enlightenment rationality and individualism happened in the wake of the scientific and industrial revolutions in Europe. It was assumed that the same could be grafted to the age old Indian civilization and a synthesis worked out. Ambedkar did not talk of a synthesis but he thought that the egalitarian ideals of the modern west was part and parcel of one of the eastern religions, namely Buddhism. He thought that Buddhism was a rational religion and had all that Hinduism lacked, namely, liberty, equality, and fraternity. But a rational Buddhism which perfectly conformed to his egalitarian ideals was **his construction** of the Buddha's message as we shall see in the next section.

We need to reckon with the fact that the efforts of the reformers to rid Hindu society of pernicious practices like Sati, child marriage, the prohibition on widow re-marriage, and generally to give women a better place in society was on the whole a failed project. Some success was achieved in banning Sati because Sati was a public act and the police could be summoned to stop it. However, cases of women committing Sati are still being reported. Though the Hindu Code Bill was passed 'in separate bits' and Nehru in his tribute to Ambedkar on his death, said that he would be remembered 'as a symbol of the revolt against the oppressive features of Hindu society and also for the great interest and the trouble he took over the question of Hindu Law Reform'

(Guha, 2004), the implementation of the law which Ambedkar drafted is at best patchy. No one can say that patriarchy among the Hindus is much less assertive now than it was before. Besides patriarchy, there are other reasons for the overall failure of the reform project. It is wrongly assumed that the educated Indian's mind opens up to liberal and egalitarian ideas once he acquires modern education. It is often not realized that education is sought and acquired for a job and barring exceptions, it does not open up the mind of the educated to liberal ideas. It seems to me that there is no greater misnomer than the phrase 'modern liberal education.' In rural India, where most of the country's population still lives, the Sanskritisation process and Sanskritic Hinduism seem to be the major hurdles to the reform of Hindu society. Those who have socio-economic status or are in the process of acquiring it, practice prohibition on widow re-marriage, seclusion of women, and of course, dowry. Child marriage is still common in rural India though it is prohibited by law.

Ambedkar and Buddhism

In 1924, Ambedkar spoke of the possibility of the depressed classes continuing in the Hindu fold to 'preserve the Aryan religion.' (Zelliot, 1998: 81). But he became increasingly bitter. His efforts to secure civic rights for the untouchables—such as drinking water and access to roads—met with opposition from upper castes Hindus. Till the mid-thirties, the dalits' efforts to enter Hindu temples at Vaikkom and Nasik also did not yield any tangible result. The Poona Pact of 1932 was a bitter pill for Ambedkar because he was pressurized to compromise to save Gandhi's life and give up his demand for separate electorates for the untouchables. On 12th October 1935, at the Bombay Presidency Depressed Classes conference near Yeola in Maharashtra, Ambedkar declared: 'I was born a Hindu and have suffered the consequences of untouchability. I will not die a Hindu'. (Omvedt, 2004: 61).

For the dalit community as a whole, ostracized and despised for generations by the Hindu upper castes, Ambedkar searched for an alternative religion which would give them a sense of belonging. He found the answer in a re-constructed Buddhism. Accordingly, he re-constructed the Buddha's message to suit the needs of his people. The concepts removed from the re-constructed Buddhism were the four noble truths and karma: the former on the ground that it was a pessimistic doctrine and the latter because it introduced fatalism and 'sapped the spirit of revolt'. To Ambedkar, Buddhism was a rational religion without any kind of superstition. This made Ambedkar take from Theravada Buddhism the concept of **pradnya** or knowledge; from Mahayana Buddhism he took the concept of **karuna** or compassion, for his people needed compassion. (Fiske and Emmrich, 2004). Hence concepts from two different schools of Buddhism were combined by Ambedkar in his re-constructed Buddhism. To Ambedkar, Buddhism was an egalitarian religion based on liberty, equality, and fraternity.

It may be argued that if social reformers like Ram Mohun Roy could interpret the Upanishads in terms of a rational Hinduism which did not sanction caste, idol worship or superstition, then surely Ambedkar had the right to interpret Buddhism to suit the needs of the dalits. Ambedkar was much taken up with the functional aspect of religion and firmly believed that in both savage and modern societies, religion fulfilled the felt needs of its adherents. The Marxian dogma of religion as false consciousness was something not worth considering for Ambedkar. (BAWS, Vol.3: 441–53; 459–62). This said, there is in Amebdkar's thought the difficulty with his assumption that the re-constructed Buddhism actually existed in ancient India. He said that in Mauryan times, the untouchables were Buddhists and they were free men. Bondage under the Hindus for the untouchables came when the Mauryas were succeeded by the Brahmin ruler, Pushyamitra Sunga. (BAWS, Vol.7: 311–20). However, research on early Buddhism suggests that even during the time of the Buddha, the society outside the sangha was not egalitarian. In keeping with the Buddha's teaching there was no caste system; but the well to do peasants and traders belonged to the upper social strata known as **unchakulas**, while the barbers, potters, and village servants belonged to the lower social strata known as **nichakulas**. (Chakravarti, 1987). In Ambedkar's re-constructed Buddhism, gender inequality did not exist and the Buddha was made to say: 'I am not an upholder of sex inequality', (Fiske and Emmrich, 2004: 111); however, there was gender inequality in the Sangha. The Buddha's close disciple, Ananda had to plead for admission of women in the sangha. The Buddha relented but women were not equal to the men. Older women had to show respect to the younger bikshus. (Chakravarti, 1987).

The competitive identity politics of colonial India based on caste, community, and religion was projected on to ancient Indian history which was re-constructed to suit diverse agendas. Thus, the work of the orientalists spoke of ancient India as a great civilization which witnessed excellent work in fields of art, Sanskrit literature, philosophy and science. This was used by the Hindu nationalists to claim that the Hindu civilization had reached great heights. It is possible that this was regarded as an upper caste appropriation of ancient Indian history. The way the leaders of lower caste movements in colonial India reconstructed India's ancient past suggests such a possibility. Phule in Maharashtra and the leaders of the Dravidian movement in south India claimed that before the Aryan invaders came from outside, the original inhabitants of the sub-continent had a glorious past. (Irschick, 1986). As noted earlier, through his own re-constructions, Ambedkar claimed a separate identity for the untouchables as Buddhists during Mauryan times and also a higher varna identity for the Shudras since ancient times. It is interesting to note that it is the later Ambedkar who is trying to establish a separate identity for the dalits through his historical re-constructions. The early Ambedkar is talking of the unity of India's culture. In his Columbia seminar paper, he said:

> I venture to say that there is no country that can rival the Indian peninsula with respect to the unity of its culture. It has not only a geographical unity, but it has over and above all, a deeper and much more fundamental-unity-the indubitable cultural unity that covers the land from end to end. But it is because of this homogeneity that caste becomes a problem so difficult to be explained... Caste is a parcelling of an already homogenous unit, and the explanation of the genesis of caste is the explanation of this process of parcelling (BAWS, Vol. 1: 5–22).

His studies of religion made Ambedkar argue that religion had evolved since ancient times. While in ancient times, religion fulfilled the needs of the community in terms of good harvests, success in wars and its welfare, in modern times, 'the concept of community and its welfare linked to God weakened' and religion became individualized based on 'justice to the individual'. (BAWS, Vol. 3: 24). This conception of the evolution of religion landed Ambedkar in a contradictory position so far as Buddhism was concerned because, in opposition to Hinduism which he perceived as caste centered, he constructed Buddhism as a religion based on liberty, equality, and fraternity. At the same time, the needs of the long suffering dalits made Ambedkar construct Buddhism as a religion which gave them a sense of belonging, promoted their identity and solidarity. Now it is obvious that religion cannot promote individual freedom and solidarity at the same time. It is worth recalling here that

Durkheim perceived the rise of individualism in the modern west as a sign of pathology which weakened the religious bonds. (Durkheim, 1897). It could be that Ambedkar's exposure to eastern and western thought and his search for an indigenous religion to which the dalits could convert, led him to contradictory positions. It is difficult to say if he was aware of these contradictions.

The Shudras and the Conquest of India

Ambedkar frequently argues in his writings that, since the Shudras who formed the bulk of the population in the country were prohibited by the Shastras from bearing arms, the country succumbed to the foreign invader and lost its freedom; he says that the Kshatriyas who alone could bear arms according to the Shastras, failed in their duty to protect the country from foreign invasions; nor could they deliver on protecting the other castes. Ambedkar does refer to caste as a system of graded inequality; but the constant reference in his writings to the conquest of India by the foreign invader due to the lowest position assigned in the varna order to the Shudra, indicates his belief that the caste system, particularly the occupational distribution of varna was responsible for India's subjugation to foreign rule. (BAWS, Vol. 9:201–17; BAWS, Vol. 1: 47–80). Ambedkar's argument is somewhat analogous to the argument of some modern Indian historians who hold the view that the 'pernicious caste system facilitated' the Muslirm conquest of India. (2).

Though there is no denying that any country which is a divided house or assigns the job of fighting to only one segment of its population, can succumb to foreign invasions, the point that needs to be raised with regard to this argument of Ambedkar is whether any consciousness of nationhood existed in India in medieval times when the Muslim invasions took place. The work of Benedict Anderson suggests that the nation is a modern concept. Further, Anderson argues that the nation is an imagined community which brings together very diverse groups. (Anderson, 1983). Since the very concept of a nation and national consciousness did not exist in medieval India, Ambedkar's argument on India's subjugation to the external invader due to the Shudras not being allowed to bear arms, is difficult to sustain.

In an essay which he wrote in 1936 on 'Annihilation of Caste', Ambedkar said that:

> There is no Hindu consciousness of kind. In every Hindu the consciousness that exists is the consciousness of his caste. That is the reason why the Hindus cannot be said to form a society or a nation. There are however many Indians whose patriotism does not permit them to admit that Indians are not a nation, that they are an amorphous mass of people. They have insisted that underlying the apparent diversity, there is a fundamental unity which marks the life of the Hindus in as much as there is a similarity of habits and customs, beliefs and thoughts which obtain all over the continent of India. Similarity in habits and customs, beliefs and thoughts there is. But one cannot accept the conclusion that therefore, the Hindus constitute as society. (BAWS, Vol. 1: 47–80).

Here clearly Ambedkar is commenting not only on what he perceives as lack of national consciousness among Hindus, but he is also making a debatable point about Hindu consciousness. It is possible to argue that Hindu consciousness did come into existence in modern times despite all the caste and class divisions. (Thapar, 1989: 209–31). If this were not so, it is difficult to account for the Rashtriya Swayamsevak Sangh (RSS) or its political Avatar, the Bhartiya Janata Party (BJP).

Returning to Ambedkar's argument about the position of Shudras and India's subjugation, military historians point out that in medieval times, what proved decisive in the battlefield was the use by the Muslims of mounted archers who could 'shoot six times before a musketeer could fire twice'. The mounted archers comprised Turks and Mongols who were trained from childhood. There was also strategic use of the infantry and the artillery. (Streusand, 2001:339–40). Hence, not allowing the Shudras to bear arms may not have contributed to the victories of the Muslims. The works of Simon Digby and Seema Alavi suggest that once Delhi Sultans, the Mughals, and later the British established their rule, these rulers maintained their supremacy through the control of the horse routes and the trade routes. (Digby, 2001; Alavi, 2001). Moreover, Christopher Bayly in his book argues that intelligence network and gathering played an important part in the British conquest of India. (Bayly, 1996).

In pre-colonial north India, sections of peasantry were the source of recruitment for the rulers during times of armed conflict. The peasants who took up arms were Ahirs, Gujars or Jats. They could be regular retainers or mercenaries. (Alavi, 2001). The Hindu recruits generally claimed Kshatriya status while the Muslim recruits claimed Ashraf status. It is obvious that there would be no need for these Hindu recruits to claim a higher varna staus if they already enjoyed it. Kolff (2001) cites Dutch records to show that the weavers in the town of Baroda in 1620 were 'usually at home during the rainy season but went to serve in the army in the dry months in the year'. This again shows that Ambedkar was off the mark when he maintained that the Shudras were disarmed owing to Shastric prescriptions. In medieval India, there was a military labour market which was drawn mainly from the peasants; the jobs included protection of caravans and resisting revenue exactions. (Kolff, 2001). The onset of British rule did not mark a major departure so far as the source of military recruitment is concerned. The peasantry in the countryside continued to be the main source for such recruitment. The British, of course, constituted a good many their army regiments on the basis of caste.

The Dalits and Hindu Society

It was Ambedkars's lifelong endeavour to forge unity among the dalits and give them a separate identity 'away from the Hindus' as he put it. The later Ambedkar (late 1920's onwards) often used the terms 'we' the untouchables and 'they' the Hindus, meaning thereby that the Hindus were the 'other' and the dalits were not Hindus. The reasons for this are obvious enough. Without unity and an ideology, his movement could not hope to achieve its goals. The dalits faced the major challenge of overcoming centuries of economic and social deprivation and this could be done only through a unified and a strong movement. Given the need to forge unity among the dalits, Ambedkar was worried about the caste divisions among them. He spent 'much time and energy thinking about this obsession with hierarchy so as to challenge it more effectively'. (Jeffrelot, 2000: 26). Ambedkar was aware that the dalits were 'infested with the caste system in which they believe as much as the high caste Hindu. This caste system among the untouchables has given rise to mutual rivalry and jealously and it has made common action impossible'. (3).

What is striking is that though the dalits generally do not have the sharp economic inequalities existing among the touchable Hindus, they have almost all the features which Hindu caste society has. If this is viewed by some as an overstatement, let us consider the following facts. First, there exists caste hierarchy among dalits. To cite a few examples: the Mahars, Mangs, Doms, and Chamars in Maharashtra, the Ezhava, Pulaya, and Cheruman in Kerala, the Chamars and Bhangis in Uttar Pradesh, the Mallas and Madigas in Andhra, all form part of a caste hierarchy among dalits. The dalit castes are endogamous and like the touchable Hindus follow rules relating to exchange of food. Jaffrelot cites a Master's thesis by M.G. Bhagat entitled *Untouchability in Maharashtra* and written in 1935; it shows that the Mahars were unwilling to take milk from the Mangs and the Chamars refused to accept milk from the Bhangis. We are also told that the Mahars in Sholapur district refused Mangs access to their village well. No doubt things have changed since the 1930's and now there is greater unity and assertion among dalits; but no one can say that caste divisions among them have disappeared. Second, like those above the line of pollution, there were and still are efforts to Sanskritise among dalits. The early Ambedkar performed the Shradh ceremony for his father (Omvedt, 2004) and did try to Sanskritise as noted earlier. Mahars like K.F. Bansode (1879–1946) and G.A. Gavai (1888–1974), tried to sanskritise the dalits. Bansode and Gavai convened a meeting in 1903 of Mahars, Mangs, and Chamars where they advocated abstaining from meat, alcohol, and employing a Hindu teacher for educating the children. (Jaffrelot, 2000: 42–43). Third, there is patriarchy among the dalits. Accounts by dalits themselves of family life in the community, refer to wife beating. The declining sex ratios among the scheduled castes and Chamars in Uttar Pradesh point to discrimination against females. In 1901, the female to male ratio (number of females per 1000 males) among the SC's in UP was 970; by 1981 it was down to 892. In 1901, the Chamars in UP had a female to male ratio of 986, but by 1981, the Chamars in UP had only 880 females per thousand males. (Dreze and Sen, 1995). Finally, just as among sections of upper caste Hindus, there is **guru parampara** among sections of dalits as Saurabh Dube's study of the Chamars of Chhattisgarh shows. The Chamars in this region known as the Satnamis recognized their Guru Ghasidas as *satnampurush*. They excluded other dalits from the sect, adopted vegetarianism, teetotalism, and had a purificatory bath before performing auspicious events. (Dube, 1992).

To be sure, there are differences between those above and below the pollution line but the commonalities are not insignificant. It is the commonalties and the need to take a holistic view of the Hindu caste system as Dumont pointed out, that leads me to suggest that despite the 'parelling of castes' as Ambedkar put it, those above and below the pollution line were part of one socio-cultural system. Dumont's suggestion that we should look at the whole and not just the part is extremely important which students of Indian society should bear in mind. He is right in saying that the field view of society is rather limiting, though the rich insights gained from fieldwork are certainly valuable. It is important to note that while the early Ambedkar talks of the cultural homogeneity of India, Dumont points to the unity of Indian culture and society. (Dumont, 1980: xxiii). The problem, however, with Dumont's analysis is that he 'valorizes ritual purity'; for him 'it is the cardinal value that defines hierarchy'. (Madan, 2006: 226). If this is so, then how do we explain caste hierarchy among dalits who were placed in a state of permanent impurity by Brahmanical Hinduism? To say that caste hierarchy among the dalits and the other common features which cut across the line of pollution is no more than mere imitation of the higher ups by the lower, is to simplify a complex social reality.

Conclusion

In this essay I tried to engage with the academic Ambedkar and debate some of his views on the Hindu caste system and religion. Given India's long history, the complexity of its society, and the fact that it is ever changing, makes it hazardous to reach conclusions with any degree of finality. The young Ambedkar in his Columbia Seminar paper admits that the subject of caste in India 'is likely to remain controversial forever' despite 'many learned disquisitions'. At that early stage, he seems open to suggestions on caste. He says: 'We must, however, guard against approaching the subject (caste) with a bias. Sentiment must be outlawed from the domain of science and things should be judged from an objective standpoint'. (BAWS, Vol. 1: 5–22). Later, due to the bitter experiences discussed earlier, there was a hardening of position in that Ambedkar spoke and wrote in strong terms about the Hindus and their caste system. Neither the later Ambedkar's scathing critique of Hinduism and its caste system nor his iconization by the dalits to which Zelliot refers (Zelliot, 2001: 129), should deter us from discussing and debating his ideas and ideals.

Notes

I wrote this essay for a book edited by Sho Kuwajima. The errors, if any, are entirely the author's responsibility, not of the editor.

1. Noboru Karashima in his work, **History and Society in South India** (2001) refers to landholding during Chola times. He points out that the non-Brahmin villages predominated compared to Brahmin villages. This would show that in Chola and later in colonial times, the major landowners in the Tamil countryside were the non Brahmins.
2. Simon Digby in his paper 'The problem of the Military Ascendancy of the Delhi Sultanate' (2001) discusses the view of modern historians like M. Habib who maintain that lower castes in Hindu society 'welcomed' the Muslim invaders as 'deliverers from upper caste Hindu tyranny'. Digby's own comment on M. Habib's perception is that 'such views make more than the briefest notice of military organization superfluous'. (p. 312).
3. Ambedkar's views on caste divisions among the dalits is discussed in C. Jaffrelot, **Dr. Ambedkar and Untouchability (2000).**

References

A. Archival Sources (Printed Records)

Govt. Records. 1879. North Western Provinces. *Female Infanticide*, Vol. V (I & II), Allahabad: North West Province and Oudh Govt. Press (cited as SRG, NWP, 1879).

B. Other Sources

Ambedkar, B.R. *Babasaheb Ambedkar's Writings and Speeches*, cited as BAWS, 17 volumes. Edited by Vasant Moon. Mumbai: Government of Maharashtra (Vol. 1.1979; Vol. 3. 1987; Vol. 5. 1989; Vol 7. 1990; Vol. 3.1990; Vol. 14. Parts 1 and 2, 1995).

Alavi, Seema. 2001. 'The Makings of Company Power: James Skinner in the Ceded and Conquered Provinces, 1802–1840' in Jos J. L. Gommans and Dirk H. A. Kolff (ed.) *Warfare and Warfare and Weaponry in South Asia, 1000–1800*, Delhi: Oxford University Press.

Anderson, B. 1983. *Imagined Communities: Reflections on the Origin and Spread of Nationalism*, London: Verso.

Bandyopadhyay, Sekhar. 2004. *From Plassey to Partition*, Delhi: Orient Longman.

Bayly, C.A. 1996. *Empire and Information: Intelligence Gathering and Social Communication in India, 1780–1870*. Cambridge University Press.

Champakalakshmi, R. 1996. *Trade, Ideology and Urbanization: South India 300 BC to AD 1300*, Delhi: Oxford University Press.

Chakravarti, Uma. 1987. *The Social Dimensions of Early Buddhism*, Delhi: Oxford University Press.

Dumont, Louis. 1980. *Homo Hieararchicus: The Caste System and its Implications*, Chicago and London: The University of Chicago Press.

Dreze, Jean and Amartya Sen. 1995. *India: Economic Development and Social Opportunity*, Delhi: Oxford University Press.

Durkheim, Emile. 1970. *Suicide*, London: Routledge and Kegan Paul (Reprint).

Digby, Simon. 2001. 'The Problem of the Military Ascendancy of the Delhi Sultanate' in Jos J. L Gommans and Dirk H. A. Kolff (ed.) *Warfare and Weaponry in South Asia, 1000–1800*, Delhi: Oxford University Press.

Dube, Saurabh. 1992. 'Myths, Symbols and Community: Satnamipanth of Chattisgarh' in Partha Chatterjee and Gyanendra Pandey (ed.) *Subaltern Studies*, Vol. VII, Delhi: Oxford University Press.

Das, Veena. 1968. 'A Sociological Approach to the Caste Puranas: A Case Study', *Sociological Bulletin*, XVII (2).

Fukazawa, Hiroshi. 1998. *The Medieval Deccan: Peasants, Social Systems and States*, Delhi: Oxford University Press.

Fiske, Adele and Christoph Emmrich, 2004. 'The Use of Buddhist Scriptures in B. R. Ambedkar's The Buddha and His Dhamma', in Surendra Jondhale and Johannes Beltz (ed.) *Reconstructing the World: B.R. Ambedkar and Buddhism in India,* Delhi: Oxford University Press.

Gore, M.S. 1993. *The Social Context of an Ideology: Ambedkar's Political and Social Thought,* Delhi: Sage Publications.

Guha, Ramachandra. 2004. 'Reforming the Hindus', *The Hindu,* 18th July.

Irschick, Eugene, F. 1986. *Tamil Revivalism in the 1930's,* Madras: Cre A.

Jaffrelot, Christophe, 2000. *Dr. Ambedkar and Untouchability,* London: Hurst and Company.

Karashima, Noboru, 2001. *History and Society in South India,* Delhi: Oxford University Press.

Kolff, Dirk H.A. 2001. 'The polity and the Peasantry' in Jos J. L. Gommans and Dirk H. A. Kolff (ed.) *Warfare and Weaponry in South Asia, 1000–1800,* Delhi: Oxford University Press.

Mani, Lata. 1998. *Contentious Traditions,* Delhi: Oxford University Press.

Mayer, Adrian, C. 1960. *Caste and Kinship in Central India,* London: Routledge & Kegan Paul.

Marriott, McKim, 1959. 'Interactional and Attributional Theories of Caste Ranking', *Man in India,* Vol. 39, No. 2.

Madan, T.N. 2006. 'The Sociology of Hinduism: Reading "Backwards" from Srinivas to Weber', *Sociological Bulletin,* Vol. 55, No. 2.

Meenakshi, K. 1996. 'The Siddhas of Tamil Nadu: A Voice of Dissent' in R. Champakalakshmi and S. Gopal (ed.) *Tradition, Dissent & Ideology,* Delhi: Oxford University Press.

Omvedt, Gail. 2004. *Ambedkar,* Delhi: Penguin Books India.

O'Hanlon, Rosalind, 1985. *Caste, Conflict and Ideology,* Cambridge: Cambridge University Press.

Parekh, Bhikhu. 1999. *Colonialism, Tradition and Reform,* Delhi: Sage Publications.

Pradhan, M.C. 1974. *Political System of the Jats of Northern India,* Delhi: Oxford University Press.

Rodrigues, Valverian. 2002. *The Essential Writings of B. R. Ambedkar,* Delhi: Oxford University Press.

Sen, Asok. 1977. *Iswar Chandra Vidyasagar and his Elusive Milestones,* Calcutta: Riddhi-India.

Singh, Natwar K. 1981. *Maharaja Suraj Mal 1707–1763,* Delhi: B.I. Publications.

Srinivas, M.N. 1952. *Religion and Society among the Coorgs of South India,* Oxford: Clarendon Press.

Srinivas, M.N. 1966. *Social Change in Modern India,* Berkeley: University of California Press.

Srinivas, M.N. 2002. 'The Cohesive role of Sanskritisation' in M.N. Srinivas *Collected Essays,* Delhi: Oxford University Press.

Stein, Burton. 1999. *Peasant State and Society in Medieval South India*, Delhi: Oxford University Press.

Streusand, Douglas. 2001. 'The Process of Expansion' in Jos J.L. Gommans and Dirk H.A. Kolff (ed.) *Warfare and Weaponry in South Asia 1000–1800*, Delhi: Oxford University Press.

Thapar, Romila. 2004. 'Imagined Religious Communities? Ancient History and the Modern Search for a Hindu Identity' in David N. Lorenzen (ed.) *Religious Movements in South Asia 600–1800*, Delhi: Oxford University Press.

Vishwanath, L.S. 2000. *Female Infanticide and Social Structure*, Delhi: Hindustan Publishing Corporation.

Vishwanath, L.S. 2004. 'Female Infanticide: The Colonial Experience', *Economic and Political Weekly*, Vol. XXXIX, No. 22.

Washbrook, David, 1989. 'Caste, Class and Dominance in Modern Tamil Nadu' in Francine Frankel and M.S.A. Rao (ed.) *Dominance and State Power in Modern India*, Vol. 1, Delhi: Oxford University Press.

Zelliot, Eleanor. 1998. 'Gandhi and Ambedkar: A Study in Leadership' in J. M. Michael Mehar (ed.) *The Untouchables in Contemporary India*, Jaipur: Rawat Publications.

Zelliot, Eleanor. 2001. 'The Meaning of Ambedkar' in Ghanshyam Shah (ed.) *Dalit Identity and Politics*, Delhi: Sage Publications.

3

Tokyo Air Raid, 9–10 March 1945 and We

Kazuko Kuwajima

I met Rajam Krishnan first in 1997 in the process of my translation of Tamil women writers' works into Japanese. The translation of her novel, *Manudatthin Maharanthangal* (Pollens of Humanity) was published in Kyoto in 2002. Since then I have been meeting Rajam Krishnan occasionally, and am always impressed by her active and sincere approach to life. It is needless to say that she is one of the prominent writers in Tamil Nadu.

When an idea of a joint work by both Indian and Japanese authors was mooted, I wanted eagerly Rajam Krishnan to join this plan. So far many interviews with her were tried, but I wanted to know specifically what led Rajam Krishnan to her writer's work, and how the Second World War had impact on her life. In this connection, I wrote a letter to her as follows:

Dear Mrs. Rajam Krishnan,

Now I am trying to write a recollection of the Second World War, as I survived the American air raid in Tokyo on 9-10 March 1945. On that occasion our family lost our house and other properties. We barely escaped only with our lives.

At that time I lived in the down town of Tokyo. That area was reduced to ashes, and many people were killed miserably by the incendiary bombs. I can recollect the scene clearly even now.

Recently the office of the city, where I live now, collected some recollections of the Second World War from those people who experienced it. I also wrote a short story, as I wanted young children to know these experiences. When the news of the Japanese attack on Pearl Harbor reached us, I was only eight years.

Now I am in the 'twilight years of my life'. Therefore I decided to write a recollection of the Second World War in more details.

In our last meeting in January this year (2005), you told me that you experienced the war and the fear of air raid in your younger age, and that it also contributed to the making of your thought. As we know well, you wrote so many articles about the problems of the society. But, if you have not yet written in details about your own experience during the war, and also how it contributed to your idea of society, literature and life, I request you to write about it for us. ——

Once I read M.G.R. (ex-Chief Minister of Tamil Nadu)'s first wife died in the midst of the chaos caused by the Japanese air raid in Chennai. I express deep sympathy with her.

I hope you will kindly take up this theme, and write about your own experience of the war and its impact on your idea.——

Yours sincerely,
Kazuko Kuwajima

The memoir of Rajam Krishnan is its result. It reminded me of the days which I spent during the Second World War. Therefore, my recollection is also attached to Rajam Krishnan's paper in this series of essays.

Both the people of Chennai, and we Japanese suffered from the air bombing during the war. But, they were forced to be entangled in the war, while Japan forced hardships caused by the war on the Asian people under the name of their 'liberation'.

I

I was born in the down town of Tokyo. When the Japanese attack on Pearl Harbor occurred on 8 December 1941, I was a second year student of a primary school. My father called together three sons and one daughter, and showed us a world map and the newspaper which reported the big news. He told us that in Asia only Japan and Thailand were independent countries, not colonized by Euro-American powers, and Japan had declared war against these powers including the USA and the UK.

I saw the map carefully, and thought how Japan could win the war, as Japan was a small country, and had only limited natural resources. I had already known American giant warships through cinema news. I never believed that Japan would win the war.

I cannot clearly recollect why I thought so. Most probably I was influenced by my mother's way of thinking, though she always took care of us nicely, and I never heard her view of the war. As I was her only daughter, I was always with her. My mother took me everywhere she went, and therefore I came to like even the women's talk which included many rumours.

One day, my mother and I went to the residence of a young poet, who was not yet famous, but became very popular after the war. She complained of the behaviour of his son who was a classmate of my eldest brother, and said in the end, 'You are a poet. So you must be able to understand what I meant'. On our way back, I asked her, 'What is a poet?' I may have been only five years old, but she answered, 'A poet is a writer of poems'. I could not understand what she told me, but said, 'Oh, I see'.

Near my house there was one of the big parks and hills in Tokyo. It is Ueno Park. During the war many tunnels were dug through the hill by Korean workers. People said the Daihonei (Military Headquarters) might come later. These workers were the people forcedly taken to Japan from Korea. They built small huts, and most of them lived with only the clothes they happened to be wearing. My mother expressed her sympathy with them, and simultaneously worried about their unclean working conditions.

Before the end of the war, all of our family were evacuated to my mother's native town in Kyushu, a big island located in the southern part of Japan. When we went to her sister's residence, we passed near by the air base, and there we saw very young men who were the members of suicide squads called Kamikaze Tokkotai. My mother explained us that they were pilots of fighters who were going to rush at American warships directly in a few days. At that time, I wondered whether there was no other choice to take for them.

I always thought that the human life was more important than the war. It was the lesson which I learnt from my mother.

II

From 8 December 1941 to October 1944 our living was comparatively 'peaceful', though it became definitely difficult due to the shortage of daily goods, rather a dearth of food, and the news from the battlefields was rather desperate. Still, battles were fought outside the territories of Japan, in the vast areas of China, Southeast Asia and the Pacific islands.

But, from November 1944 American bombers B29 attacked Japanese islands almost everyday, and many non-combatants fell victims of the war. From the late evening of the 9th March 1945 to the early morning of the 10th there was American massive aerial bombing in Tokyo. According to the American sources, about three hundred bombers dropped 1700 tons of bombs only on one night. About one hundred thousand people-men, women and children were killed. It was the Japan's biggest tragedy caused by the bombing next to Hiroshima and Nagasaki.

On that night, at first I heard the roars of bombing in the distance, and they came nearer and nearer. Finally, I heard the earsplitting sound at the nearest point. The American bombers dropped many incendiary bombs, and fire was closing in on all of my family. I and two younger brothers ran away from our house, and proceeded towards Ueno Park. The strong wind blew from north to south, and sparks of fire fell on our bodies incessantly. But, on our way to the park the incendiary bomb dropped in front of the entrance of one house, and breathed fire. We could not go straight on the street. Fortunately, on the opposite side of the house was a vacant space, where previously a pubic bathhouse was located. The owner of the house was forced to close his business due to the compulsory delivery of his iron boiler to the navy under the name of making the warships. We went round the vacant land, and could escape danger to go to the park.

By the way, this delivery of the iron goods to the government was not unusual during the war, as Japan had not enough natural resources. For example, the father of my classmate was a printer, but delivered his printing machine to the government. As the result of it, he was forced to close his shop, and his family evacuated to the countryside.

At the entrance of the park we met a boy who was about six years old. He was a son of the barber who lived near my house. He was panic-stricken and fell down there. I asked him, 'Where are your parents?' He answered, 'They asked me to run away earlier. Parents will come later'. Certainly all parents asked their children to escape first from the fire, and tried to catch up with them later. Therefore, in our locality children were saved, but rather adult and old people fell victims of fire.

A lady of a shoe shop who ran away to the park got all of her body burnt, but did not say any word of complaint. She was only anxious for the safety of her fifteen year old daughter who was expected to come after her. Next day she passed away without any complaint of her pain, as if she slept peacefully.

After two or three days many people came back to their own places. But they could not find out where their houses were. At that time, most of Japanese houses were made from wood, and everything was burnt out. We only imagined the location of our houses.

In front of my house we saw the dead bodies of an old couple. They looked like transparent wax effigies.

My eldest brother, a middle school student at that time, had a friend whose father was a seal cutter and had a shop in the main street. On that night they were staying in the countryside of Tokyo where they were helping a family whose young son had gone to war. They were looking fixedly at the sky dyed with red in the direction of Tokyo, and talked each other, 'It's a very beautiful sky'. On 10th March both came back home, but my brother's friend found none of his family members there. He made all efforts to find them out for a few days, but in vain. Most probably all of his family were burnt out. We have heard nothing from them since then.

Our locality turned into a sheet of fire, and all houses located downwind from the bombing points were burned to ashes. The residences of a painter well-known for his Japanese style painting, and a young poet earlier mentioned were also included in this area.

It is said that the temperature of fire rose up to 3,000°C. The concrete building of my primary school was also burned down. A woman teacher and her daughter died in the basement of this building. They had fled there from their house as it was destroyed by the bomb, and had taken shelter in the school.

The ordinary bombs destroyed only houses, but incendiary bombs burnt down all the houses and their belongings. It is said that American, British, and other European forces used ordinary bombs in Europe, while incendiary bombs were used in Japan because of the nature of Japanese houses made from wood.

However, even during the massive bombing we could witness the resolute will of the people here and there.

I had an elder friend. As I had no sisters, she was like my elder sister. She lived in a very spacious residence, and there was a garden on the premise. On the eastern side of the garden she lived with her parents and elder brother, and in the part separate from the main house on the western side her grandmother and aunt, a younger sister of her father, lived. The aunt was suffering from tuberculosis, the most dreaded disease during those days in Japan.

Her grandmother and aunt were always saying that, if the bomb fell down, they were sure to be killed, as there was no other place to go and depend upon. On that night an incendiary bomb directly fell on their room, and there was no response from the room, though their family members shouted loudly, 'Grandma and aunty! Come out, come out'.

I heard of this sad news after two or three days. In their death I found their firm determination. Even now, whenever I recollect them, I feel it difficult to control my tears.

III

After we lost our house, we found a shelter in a shrine near by. A Shinto priest and his people took care of us nicely. But, air raids occurred almost everyday, and all children were frightened and cried every time. Moreover, we had no food. Everything was burnt out.

Finally my mother decided to take us to her native place in Kyushu. It took 24 hours to reach there from Tokyo. During the long journey we could not take any meals. However, after we arrived at her hometown, we had enough food.

Again, from March to May 1945 there was not much change in our daily life. But, in June, the situation was getting very serious. The American army force already landed in the main island of Okinawa on 1 April, and the Japanese force was annihilated on 23 June. We got the report on Okinawa partly from newspapers, and partly from hearsay. It was widely rumoured that the American force would land in Kyushu soon, as it was nearest from Okinawa.

The men of the Japanese army were also collected in the most southern part of Kyushu. They were getting training as bombers on the cape facing the sea. They dug holes, and concealed themselves there. On the occasion of the American landing, they were expected to charge at their force with bombs at the cost of their own lives.

To this grave situation surrounding us, my mother showed her hysterical response for the first time in her life. She insisted obstinately that we should go back to Tokyo immediately, passing through the tunnel under the sea which connected Kyushu with the main island of Japan. We, four children, consoled and persuaded her forcefully that the American force might land next at Tokyo, the center of the main island. In fact, the American force had landed at the central part of the main island of Okinawa, and divided the power of the Japanese force completely. She finally acepted our firm view of the war situation. At that time we were still children, but we were forced to use whatever ability we had in order to reach the most reasonable decision conceivable.

On 15 August 1945 my father, working at an airplane factory, came back home earlier. He told us that the assembly line had already stopped working in the factory.

Hearing this, we awaited the statement of the Japanese Emperor which was expected to be broadcast on the radio at noon. After listening to the radio, my father said that the war must have ended now. I also understood that the war had ended, and found that we were relieved. But, my uncle, my mother's brother-in-law, became very angry, and said, 'Japan never loses the war. We are in the midst of the war. We must do our best.' However, the war really had ended. But it seemed that a new horizon was going to be explored from that moment. We felt we had unlimited possibility in every sphere of our life. Now we could act freely, and go anywhere we liked.

The war really forced all of my family members to pass through troubles and trials with the use of whatever capacity we had at that time, though we lost all our properties.

4

Impact of World War II in the Indian Context: Experience of a Writer

Rajam Krishnan

I

In the mid-nineteen thirties I was studying in a middle school class. Our place was neither a small village nor a big town. It was a taluq headquarter, and had a local fund hospital, two elementary schools, and a high school, in which I studied. My father taught English and Mathematics for classes in that high school. Our town was situated on the bank of River Cauvery known as *'akanda Kaveri'*(eternal Kaveri), a mile wide across north and south banks of the river. Ours was on the southern side. We had no bridges and no railway connection to go to Trichy town. We used to cross the river in a basket like boat built of bamboos and cattle hides, known as *'parisal'*. It was a very fertile place, several canals running through lush green rice fields, betel vines, vegetables and flower gardens etc.

We belonged to the Smartha Saiva Brahmin community. My father devoted his life as a teacher—a noble profession indeed. My mother was liberal in her outlook, and was more practical. They had six children. I am the second daughter, and all my four brothers are younger than me. Our parents were not so orthodox as to practice untouchability in our household. Boys belonging to the Adi Dravida community sometimes would hesitate to come to our portal, but my father encouraged them to come to his room on some errand to take a book from the shelf, or to carry the desk inside. I was not conscious of the tradition of untouchability in those days.

In the thirties, King George V passed away, and Edward VIII succeeded the throne. But owing to his love affair with a divorcee, he abducted the throne. King George VI was our king then. But, our school was not so strict as to follow the routine of singing 'God save our gracious King' in the evening before the bell was rung. On the contrary, I can cite a few instances which enabled us to awake the national consciousness in our minds.

In those days, district educational officers were white men. There would be annual inspections. Those officers normally did not visit the lower classes in the school. There was a big fuss when the officers passed through our classes in the verandah, Head Master and other officials following.

On that day, we were aware that the D.E.O. had come for inspection. I was in the sixth standard. Without any paraphernalia, that gentleman, an Indian, entered our classroom. My teacher hurriedly put his turban on his head. We all stood up. I was the only girl student studying in the class. He came near my desk, and took up the pencil from the desk, and saw the printed letters. 'H.B. Made in England'. He kept the pencil back on the desk, and took out a yellow coloured pencil from his coat pocket. 'This pencil is very good. "Congress Golden Jubilee Pencil 1935". You all should buy this *swadeshi* pencil', he said, and went back. Then, after many years, I came to know that he was a great man, Dr. S.R. Ranganathan, who was known as the father of Library Science.

Almost in the same year, the inter-district schools sports event took place in our town. Because our town was surrounded by a vast maidan, where all games could be played at the same time. That year, the Head Master called me, and told me that I should sing the invocation song before the event in the morning. I had to sing loudly in high pitch, so that entire gathering could be heard. The song selected and given was the 'Revelation'. It was Subramanya Bharathi's song hailing Tamil Nadu, glorifying its language, people, literature et cetera. In those days, nobody would dare to sing such patriotic songs in a public or government function. We did not even hear of microphones then. I practiced for four days, and sang for the opening of the morning event. It was a success. All the teachers who had come from various schools, and our Head Master in particular were very happy.

One more event is also memorable. May be in 1936, Netaji Subhas Chandra Bose came to our town. He was taken in a procession, defying Government orders. He passed through our street. We were on our doorsteps, greeting him. There were only seven or eight persons following the car, shouting 'Subhash Chandra Bose ki Jai, Mahatma Gandhi ki Jai!' Shri Bose was seated in an open car. The seat was covered with a Khadi shawl. He was there with his broad head shining.

Hitler emerged in Germany in the thirties as a dictator to bring the European nations under his control. His might and will were terrific. Austria and Poland were taken without a scratch. Soon the Nazis dropped bombs on all European territories. Great Britain had no other choice but to declare war against the Nazis. The Second World War broke out on 3 September 1939.

II

We, in India, were British subjects. The beginning of the war did not have much impact on us directly. My marriage was celebrated in March 1940. I was fifteen years of age then.

Because of the war, gold and silver prices shot up. Before, it was 13 rupees a sovereign. Usually our marriage celebrations would last for 5 days. Owing to the cost of living, the whole affair concluded in two days. In those days, there was not much demand for dowry devoid of human consideration, as is the case these days. Of course, giving dowry was considered as a traditional custom in our community. My father could not give lavish presents in gold and diamonds but he gave whatever he could.

My husband had nine sisters and two elder brothers. After my marriage in March 1940, I left my parental home for Ooty in August 1940.

My elder sister-in-law K's husband was working in the Government House, Ootacamand, and she was expecting a child then. She had two more elder children. My father took me to Ooty with the usual gifts, and left me there. I was to look after the household and children for the time being. My mother-in-law was also there for her daughter's delivery.

Then, Arther Hope was the Governor of Madras. The impact of the war was felt everywhere in the surroundings. Everybody served the King of England, as his loyal subjects. Fun shows and fêtes were organized by the government authorities to raise money for the war fund. National consciousness was absent. A shipload of children from Great Britain was received there. They were lodged in specially built homes with all facilities for education. Since lots of white people lived there, there were schools meant for whites only. For these children, additional blocks were built. There was the Royal Military School in Lovedale, in which Indians could not get admission in those days. I was in Ooty for a year or so, and then came to Madras to join my husband. He was staying with one of his sisters who was expecting her seventh child then.

My married life was not to be blissful. Two of my sisters-in-law were in Rangoon. Because of the war they had arrived by ship, with five children and were put up in the house next door. Another sister-in-law had come from Chidambaram to Madras for her third delivery with her two elder children. She gave birth to a boy, but it came to light that she was afflicted with tuberculosis. Since it was considered an infectious and incurable disease in those days, she had to be confined in a separate room, and the newborn baby could not suck his mother's milk. We rented a big house with a separate wing facing Chepauk grounds for the sick person. People fleeing from Burma, Singapore and Malaya swelled the population of the city. The younger sister-in-law's husband went to serve the war, leaving his wife and children to be in our care.

My workload those days was unimaginable. I had to monitor the T.B. patient's temperature, give medicines, and cook for the family. Every now and then I had to wash hands in disinfectant lotion. There were four children under 3, and other grown up children. A lot of visitors and guests would be coming. I had to rise early in the morning. It would be 11 p.m. by the time I could rest myself for sleep. The sleep would be interrupted with the yelling of the boy, deprived of mother's milk. We could not find any substitute. There was no fridge, no kerosene, no gas stove etc. I had to light a charcoal stove, and heat the cow's milk a little, adding some sugar before filling up the bottle. The whole household would wake up. In February 1942, one more baby was born to my Ooty sister-in-law, and, by then, her husband had been transferred to Madras.

III

It was a crucial period. Our national leaders were negotiating terms with the British regarding the transfer of power. Once, the slogan raised was, 'Don't join the war. Don't give money to the war fund.' But thousands of village youth and town people were lured to join the army. Medical and engineering personnel were not exceptions.

One of my husband's cousins was getting married then. The bridegroom's people demanded, since the boy was a staunch nationalist, that a *khadi dhoti* with silver lace should be bought for the marriage. It was more expensive than the pure silk laced dhoti. But, after the marriage the young man joined the army, without even finishing his internship as a doctor in medicine.

All our street lights wore black caps. Our windows, too, had to be covered with black sheets, so that lights could not be seen from above. Bomb proof shelters were built in all main roads and streets of the city. Voluntary personnel, trained for air raid precaution, now and then practiced mock air raids. Panic ridden people began to leave the city for good, selling their houses, concerns, et cetera at rock bottom prices. The sister-in-law and other relatives from Rangoon had settled in Burma for generations. They had no option other than to migrate to their village, where they did not have any facilities, nor schools for their children to study.

One day past midnight, we all heard the wailing sound of an air raid warning. We carried the sick sister-in-law downstairs, and settled her in the stair-case room. Another sister-in-law was there with her one month old baby. My mother-in-law, myself, and my husband plugged our ears with pieces of cotton wool and waited for the worst to occur. After two hours, the all clear signal was heard. The next morning the Government announced evacuation of the city. I remember the scene in Egmore station with surging crowd, from ticket counters to trains. The scene could easily be compared to one not so far in the future when people born and bred on this soil would leave for an unknown destiny during partition. Somehow, we found a place to rest the sick lady in the train. My husband was the only male member remaining in the family then, whose office was not shifted from Madras. Leaving him behind, we all arrived in Chidambaram. The sick lady's husband was a lawyer there.

We had secured a house nearby, so as to look after and help her. But, all the responsibilities fell upon ourselves. Her baby was here with all the other children. We had to cook her food, which my mother-in-law would carry and serve to her. Nourishing items and beverages would be prepared in our house only. There was a special injection administered for T.B. patients in those days. It was available in Kumbakonam only. That place could be reached by a three hour rail journey once in a week. My mother-in-law would take her to that town by early morning train, and would return past 8 p.m., dead tired.

We did not have amenities, such as even cooking vessels to run the family at that time. We bought mud pots, and, with minimum resources I learnt to cook and get on. I would never forget my Chidambaram days. I lived there for 5 or 6 months, but not even once did I have time to visit the famous Nataraja temple, which was close by.

Politically, also, those days are memorable. Indira Nehru married Feroze Gandhi at that time. After the simple ceremony, both went to jail. Our Rajaji differed with the views of the Congress leaders then, and resigned his membership from Congress.

In 1942, thousands of refugees from Burma walked through dangerous terrain by land to step onto Indian soil. They became sick, and many men and women with children died midway. We received a telegram from somewhere in north India, that my sister-in-law's husband from Rangoon was lying sick in a hospital, awaiting help.

My husband was transferred to the Madurai office. Meanwhile, myself, the sick-mother's child, and another elder sister-in-law went to Madurai. There was no bomb scare in Madurai.

The 'Quit India' movement was at its peak. On 9 August 1942 Gandhiji and other leaders were arrested. Thousands of young men and women from all over the country defied ban orders and went to jail. Young college students shouting 'do or die' slogans indulged in extremist activities, cutting telegraph wires, dismantling railway tracks et cetera. Following police atrocities on passive resisters, the movement became violent and curfew was imposed. Commodities like kerosene, sugar, and other essentials were not available. We burnt vegetable oil lamps and used palmyra jaggery for the child's food.

One of my husband's cousins indulged in extremist activities, using explosives for making country bombs, et cetera. One day, he went with a revolver to shoot a big grain merchant in Tanjore and was caught. He was the only son amongst four daughters. They possessed 100 acres of wetlands in the Cauvery basin. His staunchly orthodox father worked in the Delhi secretariat and was retired. This cousin was married very young and had a beautiful wife and three daughters. He was charged under the Sedition Act, for which, the death sentence was inevitable.

The parents rushed to save their son, and declared in the court that he was mentally unsound. He was sent to a mental asylum. After some years, when he came back from the hospital, he was mentally alright, but, worse, had now become a drug addict. He fathered two more children, and, while he lived in the family, made life a hell with his addiction. One day, he went out of his home to a dilapidated house in a nearby village, and hung himself there.

People who left Madras, following the Government announcement of a bomb scare, experienced a lot of difficulties, owing to the economic strain and estranged relationships of kith and kin. They all returned to Madras, with firm minds to face even the worst. My husband was again posted to the Madras office. We all came back to face the shortages and demands of the family. We took a house in Triplicane, the same area where we had lived before. Once again the sick sister-in-law and other in-laws, pregnant and demanding all help, arrived. Before the evacuation of the city, the population was three lakhs; thereafter it swelled to five lakhs. It was a period when the new rich emerged in society, flourishing with military contracts, supplying everything for the army. In residential areas, they hired houses that were turned into clothing factories for stitching military personnels' uniforms. The ugly face of black marketing emerged to rob the innocent poor and swindle us. The main streets were seen full of white and black soldiers. We could not stir out of our houses. The ration system was not introduced then. Essential commodities like rice, pulses, sugar, cloth were not there in the shops.

My husband tried his very best to admit his sick sister to the Tambaram T.B. Sanatorium. Train facilities were scarce. He had to take a day's leave to go and see her. For her admission, he had to bribe the clerk. They asked us to take back the patient after a week. Again we brought her back home and, a month later, she passed away, leaving her 15 month old child with us. Her husband came for the funeral, but he did not take the child with him. Instead, he remarried soon after.

It was very difficult to manage the household at that period. Again we had to take a big house so that the two families with their children could be accommodated. The nasty custom (devoid of any human consideration) of a brother taking up the responsibilities of his sister's commitments was prevalent in those days. Whether on happy occasions or during misfortunes, the woman to woman relationship was non-existent. The military man came home for a fortnight and went, leaving his wife pregnant.

My mother-in-law used to stand in queue for hours together to get some measures of rice and flour. That rice would be inconsumable, and was full of tiny mud particles mixed with. We did not have hulling machines in those days. I was the only person, young and strong enough to pound the rice by hand, and clean it to make it consumable. One of the children, just three years old, would rush to help me as soon as I spread the rice on the floor. Soon she would pick up all the black particles. Her health was affected: she refused to take food, and became pale. Then only we came to realize the cause: she had been putting all the mud particles into her mouth.

Once, sea water entered into the street, crossing the Marina. I did not have any idea about that, because we could not stir out of our houses in general. My husband was working in the Electricity Department, and had to work long hours from morning to night, setting right the underground cables, which were badly damaged on account of the seawater. We did not have electric supply for a week or so. At that time, one night, planes came overhead, flying low. Since the roaring sounds were different, I came out into the courtyard. We had inner court yards in the houses in those days. I was as excited as a child and called the children and my husband, "Hey, see. The planes are flying with red-green lights on!" But soon we heard the thud sounds of explosions. And then we heard more sounds from our anti-aircraft guns that were stationed on the Marina.

'Oh! They have not given notice that there would be anti-aircraft gun practice!—'

We went to bed. There was no news about bombing in the morning papers. In the afternoon, all the schools were closed. One woman was proclaiming, 'Japanese are going to bomb again. Last night they dropped bombs.'

In the evening paper there was a small column captioned, 'Madras Bombed!!' Some 4 or 5 bombs were dropped, but two of them did not explode. 4 or 5 labourers in the harbour were killed.

However, people ignored the news. They were determined to face the worst.

America dropped the destructive Atomic Bombs over Hiroshima and Nagasaki on 6 and 9 August 1945, respectively. The world shuddered. The war came to an end.

IV

The men who went to serve the war came back to swell the unemployed crowds. The government had spent a lot, constructing air strips in remote places, bomb proof shelters et cetera. These were demolished. Our wealth, labour and whatsoever potentialities we had were swindled. We experienced the acute shortage of food commodities. Rationing was introduced. Whatever grains, flour, dehydrated potato granules were imported, provided only a meager supply of essentials for the people. Our health was affected. Young and old were afflicted with scabies. Not only in the city, but in villages also, people, and children in particular, suffered. In our household, myself, my husband and all the children suffered the worst type of the malady. Our traditional medicine with turmeric and thulasi helped us a little. Hospitals, too, did not have any medicines.

In most of the families, due to economic strain, human relationship gave way to selfish motives. There arose conflicts and wordy clashes. Joint families disintegrated.

I also felt that I was caught in the web of turmoil. My health was also not alright. But I could not help but accept the life that was ordained for me. A big question made me restless. 'Why are all these things happening?' I could not find an immediate answer. I could not blame anybody responsible for these woeful conditions which prevailed in my family and elsewhere in the society. I needed an outlet. I felt the urge in me. I felt the quest to search. Words burst out as expressions but, I could not speak out.

It was a struggle in the wilderness for years together for me to emerge as a writer. I had to break silently many invisible barriers that bound a housewife in day to day life, with no literary or academic background either. Now, after more than fifty years, I have established myself in the writing field. As a young housewife, I had found the other women members of the family to be in-laws only. Human consideration, compassion, and understanding qualities were not there. This disturbed me deeply. The urge to question this condition of women was deep rooted. Wave like thoughts brought out expressions reflecting the plight of women.

In those days, I did not have the advantage of any social contacts outside the family to share my feelings and thoughts. Papers, too, were scarce then. Thanks to providence, whenever my mother-in-law returned with essential commodities like rice, sugar, cloth piece, et cetera. after waiting in long queues for hours together, she used to bring a lot of bills. There would be separate bills for each commodity. I collected them carefully and scribbled on the back sides of the bills with a pencil. It was a thrill when I found a shape in those scribblings. This practice gave me confidence. Anyway, I was very much afraid: if my in-laws found me out, what would be the outcome!

After the war, as told earlier, the Government opened centres to teach women to cook with alternate grains like semolina, dehydrated potato chips et cetera., other than rice and pulses, to cope up with the scarcity of commodities. Along with sewing, English was also taught. The organization was called Indian Women Civic Corps. They published a monthly journal, in which 80 per cent of the contents would be in English, next 10 per cent in Tamil, and another 10 per cent in Telugu. A girl from our neighbourhood, of my age, unmarried, used to come to our house with other Tamil magazines, and talk about the magazine stories with my in-laws. Whenever I had a chance, I used to turn the pages, and, in a glance, I would grasp the trend of the magazine stories. One day, when that girl came, I was alone in the house. I asked her whether I could write a story and give it to her, so that she would ask the teacher at the center whether it would be accepted for publication. The very next day she turned up, and said that it would be accepted. Some time thereafter, with the help of my school going nephew, I got hold of a few sheets of brown coloured coarse papers. He lent me his pen. I used to help him in his homework. He was a nice boy, and very much attached to me.

Because of the lack of enough housing space, our family separated from the joint household. Myself, my husband, my mother-in-law and our sister-in law, moved to a very small accomodation. Here, the neighbourhood girls made friends with me. They were also members of the IWC center.

At that time the Government gave bonuses to their employees. Till then we had not even heard the word, 'bonus'. My husband also got it. I wrote my first story in English because I was not sure if it would find a place in the allotted few pages for Tamil.

The first story entitled 'Bonus' was published. My pen name was Lekhimi. Lekhimi means pen in Sanskrit. The girl brought the magazine, and told me that I should be present for a special programme soon to be held by the Department. This organization became Women's Welfare Department. My mother-in-law permitted it. The President, Secretary and other members congratulated me, and asked me to write more and more stories. I wrote one or two articles in Tamil, which were published. I was ambitious to be known outside as a writer in popular journals. All these days my family members were not aware of my ventures.

One day, a postman brought a journal addressed to Rajam Krishnan in which my story 'Silver Tumbler' was published. I got 10 rupees as remuneration for that. So everybody in the family came to know of my other side. Everybody was happy. My mother-in-law was happy. Overnight I became an important person for her. But, I can't say that they encouraged me. I could not shirk the family responsibilities, just because I had proven my ability in other field.

Meanwhile, my husband was transferred to Ooty. As usual, my mother-in-law accompanied us. We had convenient quarters, and I had plenty of time. My mother-in-law was a jolly person by nature. She enjoyed my manuscripts and making new friends.

I became a member in various libraries and read a lot of books. I regularly wrote for magazines and Radio et cetera. In 1948, there was an announcement in the weekly *Kalki*, inviting Tamil stories for the international short story contest held by New York Herald Tribune. Immediately I wrote a short story. It was about a cowherd boy belonging to the hill folk of Nilgiris. Our house was situated on high ground, and I would be sitting outside on the green grass, watching the beautiful meadows down, where the cows—English cows— would be grazing. The boy with his scanty dress and head cloth would be sitting with a flute trying a tune again and again. He loved the animals dearly. He used to talk to them, gather cabbage leaves from other gardens, and feed them.

My story was woven around the boy, cow and the surroundings, centering on incidents which happened in the real. I sent the story, and forgot about it. One fine morning I received a telegram. My story had been selected for the contest. I had to send its English translation immediately.

That story was published first in *Hindustan Times Weekly*. It found a place in a collection of International short stories published by the Hindustan Times. That story, "Needle and Sensibility" had been translated into many European languages, which I came to know only in 1976, when I visited the Soviet Union as a Nehru Award winner. I was told that the story had been translated into Russian in 1956 by one Mr. Andrianov.

Although I had written a novel as a serial, it was later published in book form. In 1953, I was awarded the Kalaimagal Narayanaswamy Iyer prize. *Kalaimagal* had the reputation of a high literary journal in Tamil, run by famous literary personalities. This novel, entitled *Pennkural* (Voice of Women), reflected my personal experiences in a joint family household, and though not loud, it put forth the issue of the rights for women. I established my literary career with my prize winning novel. Family systems, the nucleus of human society, have been bound by various traditions mostly attributed to religion and they have not rendered justice to women. Women to women relations were always strained with dependency on male domination. My awareness developed as a quest and widened my knowledge. I studied many Indian languages—Malayalam, Hindi, a little Kannada, Marathi, et cetera. Whenever I had an opportunity I traveled a lot. I was not conscious of caste or language barriers. I lived in alien surroundings amongst fisher folks, among peasant women and others, to study their lives and struggles.

In these days, more and more women are educated, have proved their ability and talents in all fields—yet, their status in society has not improved an inch. We have to struggle for our existence. Women are considered as embodiment of Shakti as prescribed in our scriptures. But, in practice, are not treated according to human and humane values. We did not have the rights to share our knowledge and experience in decision-making areas. We still struggle to gain our rights due to us, and hope for good things to happen.

In 1983, I had the unique opportunity to participate in the World Peace Congress organized by the World Peace

Council. It was held in Prague, the capital of Czechoslovakia. About five thousand delegates representing various nations of the world were there for ten days. On behalf of the National Federation of the Indian Women I was sent as a delegate representing Indian women as well as a writer. We had a special forum for women held in the evenings. It was a rare experience for me to hear the prominent world leaders striving for world peace against war and disaster. There were women representing European countries, Latin America, Canada, Ceylon et cetera. We discussed all the issues concerning various aspects of life, our rights, progress, and development. We shared our experiences as women belonging to various strata. A nun from Philippines actually wept over the atrocities of the American soldiers stationed there, spoiling the lives of the young women of her country. Our differences of creed, colour, and language were dissolved, and our aim was only one: to save the beautiful world from disaster. We formed a human chain, and thousands of women shouted slogans against imperialism, war, slavery, and destruction. One Japanese lady, though she was very old, introduced herself to me to hold my hand. She was an activist in the Green Peace Movement. We rallied along the streets of Prague, singing 'We will overcome'.

Now 22 years have passed by since then. It has been proved that science without human concern about nature would imperil the world, and mankind in particular.

The Americans proclaim themselves as a superpower to pollute the universe from the Milky Way down to earth, causing great concern for mankind. They indulge in creating conflicts among small and oil rich nations, for their own benefits of weapon trade. Their deadly weapon trade economy flourishes, while poverty and hunger, disease and death sweep Third World countries as well as developing nations like India. Present day calamities of nature's fury—

earthquakes, floods, Tsunami et cetera., are the outcome of global warning due to the heavy pollution of gases that emanate from various factories, vehicles, and other accessories which are not essential for human well being, but, little by little, suck away the mortals of the world. We will cherish nature's bounty. Preserve the world for generations to come and live.

We have a prayer in **Atharva Veda—XIV—9—14:**

Peace Earth – Peace Atmosphere

Peace Heaven – Peace Waters

Peace Herbs – Peace Trees

May all super powers that govern the world,

Bestow peace to the world.

Peace to all – Let peace prevail everywhere

With all this peace, whenever and whatever there here, is terrible, cruel, sinful.

May all that to be tranquil, benevolent, peaceful

5

Abul Hashim— Islam, Nationalism and Democracy

Sho Kuwajima

In the beginning of the 1940s there was a trend of thought and action called the Left or the Progressives inside the All-India Muslim League. Mian Iftikhar-ud-din represented this trend in the western part of India.[1] His shift from the Indian National Congress to the League in September 1945, and his idea of Hindu-Muslim unity was criticized as fanciful by the Congress leaders. But, it was also true that Mian Iftikhar-ud-din's rather isolated battle produced a stream of thought represented by Faiz Ahmad Faiz, a poet, and Mazhar Ali Kahn, a journalist, who fought against political corruption and military regime in Pakistan. This can be observed by the history of journalism in Pakistan, and the editorials of the *Pakistan Times* in the 1950s and the *Viewpoint* in the later half of the 1970s and the 1980s.[2]

In Bengal, the Muslim League grew into the mass organization under the dynamic leadership of Abul Hashim, after he was elected as the General Secretary of the Bengal Provincial Muslim League in November 1943. His interpretation of Islam encouraged the young educated Muslims to fight against vested interests inside the League. The Dhaka League, once a citadel of the Nawab family, was challenged its leadership by the young Left leaders. The results of the 1946 provincial elections in the Muslim seats can not be conceived without taking into consideration the role of the Left in the League organization. But, the position of Abul Hashim and his Left was not so strong both among the League members of the Bengal Legislative Assembly, and also in his relations with the central League leadership. In the depths of despair he was forced to request his leave from the post of the General Secretary on 14 February 1947, though he later tried to realize his idea of 'Independent Bengal' in co-operation with H.S. Suhrawardy and Sarat Chandra Bose, from April to June in the same year.

After the Partition, the definite difference between Mian Iftikhar-ud-din and Abul Hashim in their political lives under the Ayub regime after 1958 was that, while the former's activities were severely restricted, and his *Pakistan Times* was confiscated by the military regime, Abul Hashim's idea became a part of the regime, though he often disagreed with the steps taken by the military leadership. Why it was so is worth examining.

In this paper, I seek to examine the historical role and tragedy of the thought and activities of Abul Hashim, and want to take up Mian Iftikhar-ud-din later in my separate paper. As for the political life of Abul Hashim, he left his autobiography up to the period of the Partition, though he passed away in 1974 without seeing his book.[3] Also, a biography written by Mafidul Hoque in Bangla is an excellent work with his critical view of Hashim's political life and his sympathy with the physical and circumstantial adversity of this leader, and Syed Mansur Ahmad's essay covers the familial and other background of Hashim's life[4]. Kamruddin Ahmad's clear analysis of the thought of Hashim and the movement led by him provides stimulating materials from the standpoint of the person who observed Abul Hashim closely.[5] The history of the Bengal Muslim League, written by Harun-or-Rashid and first published in

1987, is an intensive work on its organization and movement in its critical period 1940–47[6], and I used it extensively in my work on 1946 Provincial Elections in India.[7]

I

It was after November 1943 that Abul Hashim attracted educated young members of the Bengal Provincial Muslim League, though he had been elected a member of its Working Committee in 1941. The vacancy of the position of General Secretary of the Bengal Muslim League was brought by the formation of Khwaja Nazimuddin's Government in Bengal on 24 April 1943 and the entry of H.S. Suhrawardy as a minister. In the same year the Working Committee of the All-India Muslim League adopted a resolution to the effect that both the parliamentary office, like ministers and parliamentary secretaries, and the office of the League organizations would not be occupied by the same person.[8] It was Maulana Azad Subhani of Gorakhpur that proposed Abul Hashim's candidature as the General Secretary for 'preaching pragmatic values of Islam' in the League. He had known Abul Hashim since 1942, and initiated him to the philosophy of 'Rabbaniyat', which meant 'physical, mental, intellectual and spiritual development of man according to divine way of creation, sustenance and evolution of the universe visible in nature, in Al-Quran and in the life of the Holy Prophet Mohammad'.[9] However, it was the support of Suhrawardy that made a rather unknown Hashim elected as the General Secretary in the provincial League Council meeting by an overwhelming majority, despite the obstruction from the Khwaja family.[10]

Abul Hashim was born in the village of Kashiara, Burdwan District in 1905. His maternal grandfather was a Deputy Magistrate, and was later appointed Prime Minister of Bhopal. His paternal grandfather was a Class I officer of the Central Government of India.[11] Hashim's father, Abul

Kasem, did not go for any Government service, and was a devoted follower of Surendranath Banerjee. He joined the movement against the partition of Bengal, 1905. He left the Congress in 1921 when Surendranath Banerjee left it. After the Montagu Chelmsford Reforms, he was a member of the legislature, Provincial or Central, till his death in October 1936. Hashim recollects that the family did not belong to landed aristocracy, though they had a small estate in the village. He says that, though their main profession was Government service, the family had not much attraction for the life in towns and cities, which were only good for working and earning.[12] This atmosphere delicately influenced the young life of Abul Hashim. He did not enjoy his student life in Calcutta and Aligarh, though he finally passed Law in Calcutta in 1931. He returned to Burdwan very often when he could not adjust himself with his student life, and later, with his political life.

Abul Hashim was not interested in politics during his student days and during the period as a lawyer, but he formed the Young Men's Muslim Association with his classmates in 1928. At this stage, he did not want to part from the nationalist trend while feeling the necessity of a separate Muslim organization.[13] Immediately after his father passed away in 1936, thousands of people in the village and the town decided that he should lead the Muslims of Burdwan in place of his father and should be elected in the general election from the Burdwan Mohammedan Constituency.[14] Thus, he entered politics, and was elected to the Bengal Legislative Assembly in November 1936.

Joya Chatterji writes that, described in the past as 'a stronghold of Hinduism', Burdwan was one of the last bastions of the Hindu bhadralok in Bengal, and 'the epitome of the bhadralok order which the Permanent Settlement had introduced', but the 'sense of security and self-congratulation which characterized the bhadralok of

Burdwan was shaken in the following decade (1930s), when middle-class Muslims began to play a prominent part in Burdwan's public life'.[15] The appearance of a young Muslim lawyer in the political scene cannot be separately taken up from the social change in Burdwan.

Between 1936 and 1943 Abul Hashim mentions two memorable events which influenced his political life. One is his meeting with Mohammad Ali Jinnah in Calcutta in 1937, and another is the Lahore Resolution adopted at the meeting of the All-India Muslim League in March 1940.

Abul Hashim writes in his autobiography: 'Mr. Jinnah said, "Come, let us organize ourselves in such a way that we can give 24 hours' notice to the job-hunters of Bengal and the Punjab." I thought by job-hunters of Bengal and the Punjab, Mr. Jinnah meant Khwaja Nazimuddin and Sir Sikander Hayat Khan. I left him with the impression that Mr. Jinnah wanted to organize the Muslim League as a broad-based democratic and progressive political party. Believing in what Jinnah said, I joined the Muslim League. But I was deceived. Later I found that to Mr. Jinnah, persons other than Nawabs, Knights and business magnates were of no consequences.'[16]

Though Hashim did not believe in Jinnah's two nation theory, which was 'the burden of his song', the Lahore Resolution was, according to Hashim's autobiography, 'the basis of our movement for carving out of India, independent and sovereign states as homelands for the Muslims of India. It did not contemplate creation of a single Pakistan State but it contemplated two independent sovereign States as homelands for the Muslims of India. In the Lahore Resolution I saw my complete independence as a Muslim and as a Bengali and for this I supported the movement based on Lahore Resolution of 1940.'[17]

In this connection it is noted that Syed Mansur Ahmad mentions both the Islamic tradition and non-communal background of his family, and the Congress, League and Communist trends observed within the family.[18] Hashim also confesses that, outside the Legislative Assembly, his political activities were so far confined within the district of Burdwan.[19] However, no doubt the above-mentioned two events were crucial in his later political life, and cultivated Hashim's idea of 'Bengal Muslim Nationalism' and his urge to make organizational reforms in the Bengal Muslim League.

From the middle of 1943 his eyesight became poor due to *retinitis pigmento* which was caused by a blood disease in his young days. He found it difficult to walk on his own, and needed other's help for his writing and reading too.[20] Hashim talks little about this aspect except on page 35 in his autobiography, but Mafidul Hoque, a biographer of Hashim, writes that in his political life he had to pay the price for this physical handicap. It seems that both Hashim's deep attachment to the philosophy of the 'Rabbaniyat' and his daring action to reform the Bengal League organization were promoted by his strong will which tried to overcome this handicap.

Simultaneously there was circumstantial reason which needed the appearance of the new leadership in the Bengal League. In November 1943, Bengal, under the League Ministry, was in the midst of the famine. In his autobiography, Abul Hashim writes about the famine in Bengal:[21]

> During this period Bengal suffered from a severe famine. Unable to feed themselves and their children people in rural areas sold their sons and daughters. Thousands of men, women and children died of starvation. To meet the situation a Ministry of Civil Supplies was set up. Mr. Hussain Shaheed Suhrawardy was the Minister for Civil Supplies. World War the Second irreparably damaged human values and lust for immediate material values were let loose. A famine condition was artificially created by blood

suckers, hoarders, profiteers and black-marketeers. The army had priority of all means of communications for carrying army and war materials. Free movement of food became almost impossible. The government organized gruel kitchens all over the country. This was all that a Government having no control over the resources of the country could do. For proper sustenance of the people the state must have supreme right to administer the wealth when the state is independent and sovereign and this was a great lesson I learnt from the famine. In our struggle for freedom I preached this with all the emphasis that I could command.

Here Abul Hashim tries to prove that the British imperialist rule obstructed the solution of the food problems, and seems to avoid cautiously the analysis of the responsibility of the League Government and the League organization in tackling the problems, though he was actually conscious enough of the role of the Khwaja family and Hasan Ispahani in the politics and economy of Bengal.

This aspect was observed more clearly by the young League workers at the grass root level. Kamruddin Ahmad, who was working in Dhaka under the shocking scene of the famine, organized a relief committee. He noticed how negatively and reluctantly the Khwaja family and Hasan Ispahani responded to the relief movement.[22]

Under the circumstances, the appearance of Abul Hashim as a new leader of the Bengal Muslim League had a powerful impact on the thought of young educated League workers in Bengal.

II

Next day, after Abul Hashim was elected to the General Secretary, he spoke in the general session that the Muslim League in Bengal was mortgaged in three sections. One was the mortgage in 'leadership', which was imposed by the Nawab family of Dhaka or the Ahsan Manzil from the time of Sir Salimullah. The second was the mortgage of 'propaganda', which was brought by Maulana Aklam Khan's newspaper, *Azad*[23]. The third was the mortgage of 'economy', which was forced by M.A.H. Ispahani, a business magnate who was the Treasurer of the Bengal Muslim League. Hashim promised to liberate the League from these three mortgages, and provide proper place to the Muslim middle class.[24] Though the old leaders understood that these words came from a person who did not know politics, it encouraged young Muslim activists in Dhaka who were dissatisfied with the present League leadership.

Later, Abul Hashim's speech in Siraj-ud-Daulah Park, Dhaka was also rather different from those of the then leaders of the League. In Hashim's thought, Islam was not only religion, but also the way of economic and social liberation. Thus, Hashim became a leader of young educated Muslims, while the older people thought that Islam was the religion of God, which left no room for the talk from the scientific point of view.[25] Getting inspiration from Abul Hashim's thought and action, the League office called 'Party House' was started in Dhaka on 1 April 1944, and, after the struggle in the presidential election was settled, the Dhaka District Muslim League was 'liberated from the prison of the Khwajas', and started working under the leadership of the Left.[26]

While analyzing the process of the 'democratization of the Muslim League' in Bengal, Harun-or-Rashid explained that 'the college and university educated middle class romantic youths born in the 1920s, largely constituted Hashim's cadre of workers.'[27] He also clarified that, though in the eyes of the Khwaja group they were communists, and it was also true that a number of communists like Mohammad Toaha (Noakhali) and Shamsuddin (Dhaka) had infiltrated into the League organizations, the majority of Hashim's workers like Sheikh Mujibur Rahman and Khondkar Mustaq Ahmad were innocent of any such connections.[28]

How the organization, finance, and style of work of the Bengal Muslim League were radically changed is described in detail in Hashim's autobiography. From May to August 1944 Abul Hashim had an extensive lecture tour to East and North Bengal. He confirms that, with the exception of the district of Faridpur and Comilla the leftist workers of the Muslim League had full support of the people in their campaign for democratization of the Muslim League. He also admits that, while in Comilla, the leftists under the leadership of Khondkar Mustaq Ahmad, then a student, faced 'peaceful and constitutional' obstruction from the Khwaja group. Sheikh Mujibur Rahman, who was sent to Faridpur, had 'of necessity to meet violence with violence' due to the 'un-constitutional and violent methods' which this group adopted.[29]

The annual meeting of the Council of the Bengal Provincial Muslim League on 17–19 November 1944 was the place of both stock-taking and tightrope walking on the Left and the Right of the League.

In his report of the activities of the Bengal League, Abul Hashim declared that it had more than half a million formal members in 1944; 160,000 from Barisal, 105,500 from Dhaka, 60,000 from Faridpur, 50,000 from Noakhali, 44,700 from Tippera, 41,000 from Mymensingh, 40,000 from Chittagong, 24,500 from Dinajpur, 13,470 from Rangpur, and 2,000 from Jangipur subdivision, Murshidabad district.[30] In the *People's War,* a Communist organ, Nikhil Chakravarty mentions the reasons why the Bengal League became strong in one year. According to his analysis, one is the fact that the Bengal Muslim League 'has grown out of its old shell of mere communalism into a powerful organ of freedom'. Another reason was:

> the terrible experience of the famine, in the course of which the League Ministry played a timid role, has convinced the younger generation of the Muslims that the only way to make the League

strong is to go out among the people and not to exhaust one's energy in the precincts of the Legislature.[31]

Here, too, the dissatisfaction of the young Muslim workers with the League Ministry in tackling the problems of hunger is mentioned as the background of the growth of the Left inside the League. However, Abul Hashim honestly admitted in his report that the League could not make any contact with innumerable illiterate Muslims.[32] In this Council meeting, Abul Hashim's position as the General Secretary was intact despite the serious attack from Khwaja Nazimuddin and others that Hashim preached communism under the cover of Islam, and that his design was to convert the Muslim intelligentsia of Bengal to communism.[33]

But, Suhrawardy could pose himself as a balancer between the Left and the Right, and could maintain the unity of the League by forcing Hashim to swallow a list of the members of the Working Committee in which Khawaja Shahabuddin, a member of the Khwaja family was included. At that stage of the drama Suhrawardy was still 'the effective leader of the rising middle class', and Hashim was his choice.[34]

In spite of his unstable position in the League organization, Hashim's style of action attracted young Muslim workers. Recollecting his daily work at the Muslim League Party House, Wellesly First Lane, Calcutta after the shift of his residence there in December 1944, Hashim writes:[35]

Every day I had to interview hundreds of visitors coming from all parts of Bengal. The flow of visitors was almost continuous. At night I discussed with young leaders and workers of the Muslim League fundamentals of Islam, methods of party organization and political warfare, philosophy and sociology. Generally I retired to bed at 2–30 a.m. Sheikh Mujibur Rahman attended my night classes but he had little or no interest in academic discussions. He often fell asleep and rising in the morning he would ask me what was to be done. I found in him an exceptionally good young man of action and not of thought. He did his duty with precision. I taught them what I call my grammar of political warfare. I insisted on developing an attitude of tolerance towards others' views and through understanding of their own ideology. Consolidation of their own party firmly based on their ideology, seeking allies, as many as they could, neutralizing those whom they failed to secure as allies, taking the wing out of the sail of their opponents, convincing them that they stood for a wrong cause and finally, singling out their enemies and to beat them in pitched battles—these were the cardinal principles of my grammar of political warfare.

As long as his constant contact with young educated workers was maintained, Hashim's idea had a great impact on the thought and work of these people, and contributed a lot to the growth of the Bengal Muslim League, though this 'democratic upsurge' failed to affect the upper echelon of the party.[36] The strength of the Left in Bengal was shown in the Draft Manifesto of the Bengal Provincial Muslim League published on 24 March 1945.

The Council meeting had decided to prepare the Manifesto of the Bengal Muslim League following a precedent of the Punjab Muslim League. Abul Hashim prepared its draft with the help of Nikhil Chakravarty, a communist who was following the growth of the Bengal League with sympathy. However, Hashim recollects that the draft was based on universal values of Islam preached and practiced by the prophet of Islam and his faithful followers.[37]

In the draft, while expressing the establishment of Free Pakistan in Free India as its objective, the Bengal Provincial Muslim League laid emphasis on its primary responsibility of striving for the political, economic, social and moral uplift of the Muslims who formed the dominant nationality of Eastern Pakistan, but made it clear that its struggle of Pakistan was directed not against the Hindus or any other non-Muslim people. It says clearly, 'The sovereignty of East

Pakistan shall be vested in the people. A democratic state shall be set up in a Constituent Assembly elected through universal adult franchise.'

The draft Manifesto mentioned the rights of workers, peasants, artisans, women, and minorities. It is noteworthy that the draft mentions both Islamic universality and the individuality of East Pakistan as follows:

> It shall be the duty of the Muslim League to see that the principles of the laws of *Shariat* are applied and observed in Muslim society. The Islamic moral values have to be resuscitated and the tenets of Islam have to be followed. The regeneration of Islamic culture as it has developed through centuries in this land of Eastern Pakistan—its history, its folklore, its art and music shall be particularly encouraged and popularized.

Lastly, the draft promised the restoration of prosperity in villages, anti-hoarding drives and preparation for the post-war planning under the situation of hunger and disease in Bengal, and reiterated that imperialism was the common enemy of the people.[38]

This document is a milestone in the history of the League Left in Bengal, and tries to connect Islam as the inspiring idea for educated young Muslims with an image of the people-oriented state of East Pakistan.

Hashim knew well his strength and weakness in the League organization. He 'perfectly well' knew that the Working Committee of the Bengal Provincial Muslim League would never place their thumb impression on the draft Manifesto, and decided not to place it before the Working Committee for their consideration but to place it before the Council. Hashim published it on his own, but Suhrawardy questioned his authority to publish the draft and demanded disciplinary action against him. Hamidul Huq Choudhury, a member of the Working Committee, remarked that the word 'Manifesto' was a communist term.[39]

In his recollection, Hashim concluded: 'The Manifesto took the wind out of the sail of all critics of the Muslim League. It broadened and enlarged the outlook of the followers and supporters of the Muslim League and it convinced them that they were struggling for a just cause.'[40] The copies of this Manifesto were sold as one of the League publications on the occasion of the ninth session of the All India Kisan Sabha held at Netrakona (Mymensingh) on 5–9 April 1945.[41] How this literature was read among the League workers still needs careful examination.

Mafidul Hoque evaluates the meaning of the publication of the Manifesto highly, saying that it neither referred to the communalism based on the two-nation theory, nor to the secularist theory of nationalities, but it was an exceptional document during this period of upheaval in religious political consciousness.[42] The Manifesto was neither a 'communal', nor a 'secularist' document, while carrying the realization of 'a democratic State' as its objective. The period from November 1943 to the first half of 1945 was in the heyday of the activities of Abul Hashim and the League Left in Bengal, and the Manifesto was its expression.

III

On 15 July 1945, the All-India Muslim League demanded that fresh elections to the Central and Provincial Legislature should no longer be delayed and immediate steps should be taken to hold them as soon as possible. The Pakistan issue was the one point of the most intense confrontation between the League and the Indian National Congress in their election campaigns. This forced the thoughts and actions of Abul Hashim to face upon scrutiny both in Bengal and at the all-India level.

On 6 September Abul Hashim published his press statement titled *Let Us Go to War*, and asked the League members to prepare for the elections because, he said, the ballot box was the only medium through which public opinion could be ascertained with the greatest possible accuracy. He claimed that the Pakistan scheme of the All-India Muslim League represented the views of the entire body of Muslims of India. He also appealed to the League members to 'bundle up all their differences and to preserve them if necessary in cold storage during the pendency of our common struggle'.[43] But, squabbling continued between the Right and the Left, sometimes even with hand-to-hand scuffles.[44] In the selection of the members of the Parliamentary Board, Hashim's group and Suhrawardy's group occupied more than half of its seats, and Nazimuddin's group was defeated. Later, Suhrawardy showed his reconciliatory gesture to Nazimuddin and Hasan Ispahani, a right hand man of Jinnah in Bengal, with the provision of the posts of the President and Treasurer of the Election Fund Committee. The nominations of the League candidates by the Provincial Parliamentary Board were also forced to reconsider in favour of the Nazimuddin group by the final decision on the side of the Central Parliamentary Board of the Muslim League. However, Harun-or-Rashid evaluates the meaning of the victory of the Hashim-Suhrawardy group as follows:[45]

> The election to the provincial Parliamentary Board was not simply a leadership race between Nazimuddin and Suhrawardy. It was far more significant. The success of the Suhrawardy-Hashim group marked a victory for the Organization against the Parliamentary coterie. The verdict of the League Council heralded the prominence of the middle class whose representatives comprised the majority. Furthermore, it was tantamount to a vote of no confidence in Jinnah's confidants in Bengal.

In this connection the Communists who had been observing the growth of the Left with sympathy came to observe the same situation critically, saying that the entire propaganda of the Progressives harped on a mere anti-

Ministry tirade, which was soon reduced into a factional attack on the Nazimuddin group without harnessing the League to the immediate service of the Muslim people, though two years ago they came forward voluntarily at considerable personal sacrifice. They thought that the League Progressives now did not constitute a unifying force inside the League, more so because of their unfortunate participation in the squabbling at the top, and tragic negligence in serving the Muslim millions as such.[46] Not only the candidature of Communists in the Muslim seats, but this observation seems to have estranged Hashim and the League Progressives from Communists.

The incident that made the name of Abul Hashim most conspicuous in the history of the Pakistan movement is the point of order he raised in the Subjects Committee in the Convention of the League Legislators, which was held in Delhi on 7–10 April 1946, following its 'victory' in the elections. The proceedings of the Subjects Committee seem to be not yet opened to research, even if they exist.[47]

Nevertheless, there is little difference in the description of the conclusion reached through the discussion in the Subjects Committee among various political commentaries and researches. Abul Hashim said that the Lahore Resolution of 1940 contemplated two independent and sovereign Pakistan states and homelands for the Muslims of India.[48] Through the discussion between Jinnah and Hashim it was clarified that the expression of the creed of the League in the Lahore Resolution of 1940, 'independent states' in which the constituent units shall be autonomous and sovereign, stood, and the Convention was not in a position to amend the Lahore Resolution. However, Jinnah conceded only to the extent that 'one sovereign independent state' in the Resolution of the Convention should be modified into 'a sovereign independent state', which meant, according to Jinnah's explanation, one constituent assembly for Muslim India.[49]

Except the letter 'a', the only modification done in the resolution of the Convention was the omission of the preamble of the resolution. According to Kamruddin Ahmad, the preamble was vehemently opposed by Mian Iftikhar-ud-din, G.M. Syed, Abul Hashim, and Hasrat Mohani. But he also adds that Suhrawardy, while moving the resolution, used almost the same language when he placed the resolution in the open session of the Convention.[50]

So far as the demand for an independent Eastern Pakistan is concerned, Abul Hashim's protest was a lonely voice, though there is a different interpretation on the role of Suhrawardy in the Convention.[51] And, even Abul Hashim felt it difficult to resist the impassioned mood of the Convention under the background of the League's 'victory' in the Central and Provincial elections. Hashim recollects that he deliberately kept himself absent from the open session of the Convention,[52] but the *Dawn* carries his speech, though his name is misspelled as Abdul Hashim, in which the General Secretary of the Bengal Provincial Muslim League described Jinnah as the world's greatest realist, and said that Bengal was ready for any action that might be taken for the achievement of Pakistan.[53] Later, Mafidul Hoque clarified that the explanation of this speech was carried in Hashim's paper *Millat,* 19 April 1946, and Hashim said in his speech that he supported this historical resolution as a servant and fighter of East Pakistan, though he added that the independence of Pakistan meant the right of autonomy for all nations and the struggle for Pakistan meant the struggle for democracy. Hoque explained that Abul Hashim was also forced to drift in the full flush of the victory of the elections.[54] Despite this, it seems undeniable that Hashim felt isolated from the main trend at the center and in Bengal. This isolation drove Hashim to his intensive study of Islamic thought.

The elections, the Delhi Convention, and the birth of the Suhrawardy ministry in Bengal on 24 April 1946 had serious impact on the thought and work of Abul Hashim and the Left in Bengal. After his return from the Convention, he called a meeting of the provincial League workers in his village Kashiara, and asked that nobody should make their personal demands to any minister. Workers should work only for the welfare of the people through the League organizations. Kamruddin Ahmad says that most of the workers, who had then become leaders, did not listen to it.[55] As one of the Left in the League, he observes the development of estrangement of Hashim with Suhrawardy and the Left workers as follows:[56]

After the resounding victory in the General election in Bengal the leading workers of Abul Hashim inclined more towards metaphysical discussions than to organizational work. They talked about 'Rabubyat' and 'Rabbanyat' and held philosophical discussions under the guidance of Allama Azad Subhani. The rank and file were not interested in those learned debates but would not say so because they did not want to displease Abul Hashim. The leaders of the workers who made their mark as organizers of great ability soon began to function as a pressure group on the Government. They would ask for the transfer of any officer from any place if that officer would not listen to their requests. Ministers were very often threatened with dire consequences. They did not even spare the Prime Minister. Gradually misunderstanding began to grow between Abul Hashim and Suhrawardy. Most of the so-called star workers lost their ideals and were after money, and they know of no other business except selling permits, especially the Civil supply permits. They were no more the same political workers, who had organized the democratic fight against the reactionary forces in Bengal. The student community as a whole began to lose confidence in Abul Hashim and his followers.

Abul Mansur Ahmad records in his autobiography an interesting discussion with Abul Hashim. When this talk took place is not clear, but this conversation tells something of the direction of the thought of Abul Hashim who was disgusted with the opportunism and corruption of political leaders and workers.[57] Mansur Ahmad 'provoked' Hashim in his discussion by saying, 'You like Islam. I like Muslims.' After a few days, Hashim answered, 'I not only don't like Muslims, but hate Muslims.' Ahmad said, 'That means you like medicines, and hate patients.' Hashim, a man of wit, answered, 'Why don't you hate patients who spoil efficacious medicines?' It is not clear whether this was one of the 'metaphysical' discussions. But, here we feel it difficult to find a sign of his people-oriented programs which he tried to develop for some time after he became the General Secretary of the Bengal Muslim League. This discussion reflected the fact that Hashim did not place a high value on the League leaders and workers.

The first half of 1947 was the year when Abul Hashim was forced to realize that he was completely isolated though he had been so far surrounded by his followers who 'misguided' him.[58] The tragedy started with the candidature of Abul Hashim for the president of the Bengal Provincial Muslim League, immediately after the resignation of Maulana Akram Khan from this post in early November 1946.[59] Later Fazlur Huq, who returned to the League in September 1946, expressed his wish to stand as a candidate for the election to the President on 31 January 1947. Though Huq may have stood from his own wish, his candidature was fully utilized for the campaign against Hashim by the Khwaja group. Finally the Khwaja group 'betrayed' Huq, and got the support of the Council meeting in favour of the request for the withdrawal of the resignation of Akram Khan.[60] What disturbed Abul Hashim was the 'neutral' posture of Suhrawardy in this election for the President, though Hashim was 'known as the ministerial candidate'.[61] This estranged the relations of Hashim with

Suhrawardy irreparably, though both worked together for a 'united independent Bengal' after some time. Abul Hashim, who was disgusted with the situation, submitted his leave from the work of the General Secretary on 14 February 1947, and left for Burdwan. This leave was received as 'a blessing in disguise' by the Khwaja group. 'His retreat from the battlefield in this way was a politically great mistake'.[62] Kamruddin Ahmad writes about the historical meaning of this drama as follows:[63]

> It was the conspiracy of the reactionary group, and particularly of Khwaja Shahabuddin. Two tigers became preys with one shot. The Left young community was divided by the rivalry between A. K. Fazlul Huq Sahib and Abul Hashim Sahib. Fazlul Huq Sahib faced again his expulsion from politics for seven years, and Abul Hashim Sahib's political life ended.

Kamruddin Ahmad and other Leftist workers persuaded Hashim that there was no room for 'sentimentality', and if he left politics, people would forget his contribution to Muslim politics in the past three years. But, Hashim no longer listened to their advice, and left them. Later, Hashim's group of workers shifted their center of activities to Dhaka, where they 'decided to draw the attention of the people of East Bengal to the realities of life'.[64]

On 11 March 1947 the Working Committee of the Bengal Provincial Muslim League approved Hashim's leave till 15 June 1947, and instructed Habibullah Wahar to do the work of the General Secretary in the meantime. Thus was completed the system which removed Hashim from the leadership.[65]

His last efforts for 'a united independent Bengal' in Calcutta after his return from Burdwan in April, were made under this unstable position. Already much has been written about the situation around the movement for an independent Bengal,[66] and therefore I may mainly discuss the role of Abul Hashim in the movement.

As the partition of the sub-continent had become inevitable, the Working Committee of the Indian National Congress proposed the division of the Punjab into a predominantly Muslim province and a predominantly non-Muslim province on 8 March 1947. Later, Acharya Kripalani, the Congress President, stated this principle of division would apply also to Bengal.[67] The Bengal Provincial Congress Committee and the Bengal branch of the Hindu Mahasabha supported the partition of Bengal respectively on 4 and 6 April. The business leaders and historians also supported this move, and the Congress and the Mahasabha started the joint work for this campaign.[68] In this situation Suhrawardy announced his idea of 'independent Bengal' at a press conference. Two days later Abul Hashim published his press statement, and submitted his idea of an independent Bengal on the basis of the Lahore Resolution:[69]

Partition of Bengal bears no analogy to the partition of India. The lamentable perversion in thinking which suggests that the movement for the partition of Bengal is convenient counterblast to Pakistan arises out of a colossal ignorance of the content and implications of the Lahore Resolution to which and which alone and not to this interpretation or that interpretation thereof, Muslims of India owe allegiance.

It (the Resolution) merely demands complete sovereignty for those countries which are known to the world as Muslim majority countries, and by implication demands complete sovereignty and self-determination of all the nations and countries of India. It gives Bengal and other cultural units of India complete sovereignty.

— It is unthinkable that in a free Bengal, the Hindus of Bengal who constitute nearly half of its population will be denied their legitimate share in administration and in the enjoyment of other material resources. Hindu-Muslim population of Bengal is almost balanced. Neither community is in a position to dominate the other. If Bengal is permitted to harness all her resources for the exclusive service of the children of her soil, both Hindus and Muslims shall be happy and prosperous for many a century to come.

— Mr. C.R. Das is dead. Let his spirit help us in molding our glorious future. Let the Hindus and Muslims of Bengal agree to his formula of 50–50 enjoyment of political power and economic privileges.

Here Hashim seems to have adopted a more practical approach, though his idea already tilted to the philosophy of 'Rabbaniyat'. The expressions like the observation of the laws of *Shariat* in Muslim society and the resuscitation of the Islamic moral values in the draft Manifesto at least do not appear here.

When some critics questioned his authority to publish his statement, he refuted, 'No authority is necessary for a good thing. In my statement I addressed both Hindus and Muslims and did not speak on behalf of either.'[70]

The move for an independent Bengal was crystallized in the form of the Agreement for the Free State of Bengal reached in the meeting attended by Suhrawardy, Hashim, Kiran Shankar Roy, Sarat Chandra Bose, and other leaders at the residence of Bose on 20 May. The Agreement mentioned, as one of its terms, the election to the Bengal Legislature on the basis of joint electorate and adult franchise, with reservation of seats proportionate to the population amongst Hindus and Muslims.[71] Here, I will not come to the details of the destiny of this Agreement, how it was shelved by both central Congress and League leaders. Though Gandhi listened to Sarat Bose's appeal, he was not powerful enough to reverse the course taken by Sardar Vallabhbhai Patel, who was the main architect of the partition of Bengal.[72] Harun-or-Rashid analyses that at a certain stage Jinnah thought it 'much better' to allow Bengal to remain united and independent than to have a divided Bengal with its most prosperous part including the muchcovetted Calcutta city joining the Indian Union, but he was also opposed to joint electorates provided under the terms of agreement, and feared that Bengal would take the course of a secular state, and not remain a potential ally of Pakistan 'with the preponderance of the Hindus and the total unreliability of Suhrawardy and Hashim'[73]. Finally, the Working Committee of the Bengal Provincial Muslim League adopted a resolution on 28 May that Jinnah 'alone had the authority to negotiate and settle the future constitution on behalf of the Muslims of India as a whole and the Muslims of Bengal shall stand by his decision', and the sub-committee appointed for negotiations with Bengali leaders was dissolved.[74]

Later Suhrawardy did not defy Jinnah, sensing that there would be no chance of United Independent Bengal against the 'adamant' attitudes of Nehru and Patel, whatever postures Bengali Hindu leaders took.[75] Harun-or-Rashid concludes that the most formidable reason for the failure of the move was the Congress veto.[76] But, it cannot be denied that, despite his last efforts for the realization of the thought of the Draft Manifesto, by this time Abul Hashim had lost his group of workers on his side whom he trained with his mission since November 1943. Therefore, the movement for an independent Bengal could not sustain an adverse wind with its mass basis. Also, it was not only the problem of the political approach of Hashim, but here was the shadow of the political situation after Calcutta killing on 16 August 1946 on the people's movement in Bengal. The isolation of Abul Hashim was almost completed.

The meeting of the Council of the All India Muslim League was opened in New Delhi on 3 June 1947, and they accepted the Mountbatten Award. According to Hashim's recollection the Council members from Bengal met at Suhrawardy's house, and decided unanimously to oppose the official resolution if the Muslim League accepting the

Mountbatten Award. But, in Delhi, Suhrawardy supported the resolution, and Hashim and Hasrat Mohani were not allowed to speak. In the evening of 3 June, Hashim issued a press statement, saying that the decision of the Council of the Muslim League was the result of three fears: firstly, habitual fear of Mr. Jinnah; secondly, fear of an uncertain future; and thirdly, fear of their uncertain status in Pakistan if they incurred the displeasure of Mr. Jinnah.[77] The *Dawn* soon carried the editorial titled 'A Snake in the Grass', and blamed Hashim, saying that he 'has not only fallen foul of the Qaede-Azam but also given expression to certain views which are diametrically opposed to the fundamental principles which have always guided the policy of the Muslim League'. This editorial concluded, 'in our view Mr. Abul Hashim should be forthwith expelled from the League organization. It would be a good riddance'.[78]

In 1947 Abul Hashim lost not only his eyesight, but also his dream, which he had described in the Draft Manifesto and had tried to realize through his cooperation with the move for an independent Bengal. On the morning of 15 August 1947 Hashim attended the Independence ceremony in Calcutta when the Indian National Flag was hoisted on the Government House and C. Rajagopalachari was installed as Governor of West Bengal.[79] In the afternoon he visited Sodepur Ashram to meet Gandhi. Gandhi said to Hashim, 'You could not resist partition of Bengal. This is your defeat, but I assure you that you could succeed if you had not lost your vision.' Hashim commented in his book, 'By 1947 I became almost completely blind. Here he referred to the loss of my eyesight.'[80] From his own experience, Gandhi wanted to show his sympathy for the 'defeat' of Abul Hashim who was forced to allow other political leaders to act in their own way. Gandhi also expressed his deep frustration and said:[81]

The world knows Sardar Patel is my 'yes-man', but these days he says 'no' to everything I say; Babu Rajendra Prashad goes out with me in my morning walk but when I come back to my Ashram I feel as though, we shall never meet again; Pandit Jawaharlal Nehru is really a jawahar (jewel) but at times, in sentiment and emotion he makes utterances which he should not do. But he has the courage to admit his mistakes, if he is convinced otherwise. How long shall I live to see these things.

Abul Hashim also noticed that Gandhi deeply realized the defeat of his lifelong struggle. On the day of India's independence, there was something which aroused a response in each other's heart, though the context was different for the two. However, though he resided in India for some years after the partition, Abul Hashim's belief in the theory of multi-nationalism as the way to solve South Asian political problems remained, while maintaining his critical view of one or two nation theory.[82]

IV

After the partition of India, he remained in Burdwan, his father's land, and acted as an opposition leader in the West Bengal Legislative Assembly. But his main concern was now occupied with the development of his idea of 'Rabbaniyat'.

The communal riots in West Bengal in February 1950 changed his destiny. In Burdwan he had more friends among the Hindus than the Muslims. But, his house was set on fire by the students and refugees, and he was forced to cross the border into East Bengal with his family, and settled in Dhaka.[83]

By this time Abul Hashim's idea itself much departed from his earlier thought which attracted young educated Muslims in 1943–45. In his first book published in 1950, Hashim declared, 'Time has now come for the re-appearance of the spirit of religion in the full-flood of its pristine glory'.[84]

He thought the Arabic word, 'Rabbaniyat', which meant 'divincly ordained natural philosophy of creation, sustenance and evolution of the Universe', expressed the true spirit of religion.[85] Maulana Azad Subhani, who led Hashim to this idea in earlier days, wrote in the Foreword of this book, 'The philosophy of 'Rabbaniyat' runs throughout the book from cover to cover although there is a direct mention of it only in one place viz., the article on the conception of religion'.[86] He also added that philosophy of 'Rabbaniyat' was a revolutionary philosophy, but the task of showing, in concrete terms, how to mold the minute details of the everyday business of life of modern civilized society in the light of 'Rabbaniyat' was not the job of ordinary mortals.[87]

At this stage, Abul Hashim was critical of Parliamentary Democracy, and, after his analysis of the procedure of the selections of the Caliphs, showed his idea of 'the selection of the best men as leaders' as an alternative:[88]

> Democracy of Islam is just and equitable distribution of rights and privileges of the state but not equal participation of all in the affairs of the state; it gives absolute freedom of discussion but demands obedience to the decision of the good and the efficient so far as it is consistent with the Will of God or the completely unified knowledge of creation, sustenance and evolution of man.
>
> Here, as also in other matters, the admirers of Western Parliamentary Democracy try to adjust Islam with wisdom of the West and lay much emphasis on the decision of the majority and advocate the omnipotence and omniscience of the judgment and the will of such a majority. According to this conception of democracy a state is a machinery through which the will of the majority is expressed. A glance at the procedure of the selection of the Caliphs will clarify the issue.
>
> Nomination, resignation and subsequent election of Umar (RT.) II clearly show that Islam cares more for the motive than for the procedure of selection of leaders. Whatever procedure may be suitable for the selection of the best men as leaders is valid in Islam. The motive for the selection of the best men must be

uniformly present in every case but the method and procedure of selection may vary according to varying circumstances.

From this description it is difficult to imagine Abul Hashim as a leader who fought for the 'democratization of the Muslim League'. Even as Abul Hashim is said to have indirectly influenced the preparation of the draft manifesto of the Awami Muslim League, which appeared in June 1949, through Shamsul Huq who stayed in Burdwan,[89] and *The Creed of Islam* was a book of 'revolutionary philosophy', here is no place for the activities of young educated Muslim leaders who once earnestly supported Hashim's idea and movement, and the 'ordinary mortals' of Bengal as the nucleus that carries out revolution, do not appear in his thought.

Hashim's idea was an expression of the real position which he faced when he reached Dhaka. Erstwhile supporters of Hashim were divided politically, and Hashim, himself, lost his earlier passion for political movement. He found himself isolated in Dhaka. But, according to the advice of Kamruddin Ahmad, he joined the Tamaddun Majlish (Cultural Organization), and, as he was an earnest member, Hashim became one of the leaders of the language movement in 1952.[90] This Islamic organization was started by some young intellectuals and students of the Dhaka University on 2 September 1947; it campaigned for making Bangla the medium of education and legal proceedings during the first phase of the language movement.[91]

On 27 January 1952, Khwaja Nazimuddin, Prime Minister of Pakistan, made his speech in Dhaka, and declared that the state language of Pakistan would be Urdu.[92] On 31 January the All Party National Language Action Committee was formed, and Abul Hashim joined it as its member.[93] On 4 February this committee decided to call a province-wide general strike on 21 February, and Abul Hashim and other members resolved to continue the struggle until Bangla was recognized as the state language of Pakistan.[94] On 20 February Abul Hashim presided over the meeting of the committee. While the meeting was going on, the announcement was made that for thirty days from 20 February the District Magistrate of Dhaka had imposed Section 144, banning meetings, processions et cetera. in Dhaka. The majority of the members including Abul Hashim pleaded for peaceful agitation without violating the governmental order. They argued that the violation of the governmental order would provide the government an excuse for the suspension of the election, which would be a greater stake for democracy.[95] It is interesting to note that Abul Hashim, who had earlier criticized Parliamentary Democracy, supported the struggle for democracy. Government repression and the fear of the radicalization of the movement forced Hashim to return to the mainstream of the language movement and take up the posture as a defender of Parliamentary Democracy for some time. It is well known how the movement developed and how police firing happened on 21 February. Here, it is enough to cite the fact that, when a meeting of the All-Party National Language Action Committee was held on 23 February, 'the Committee had little effective role to play in respect of the movement'.[96] Abul Hashim was arrested on 25 February 1952, and came out of jail on 5 June 1953.

While Hashim was in jail, some followers of Hashim's idea decided to organize the Khilafat-e-Rabbani Party (Divine Sovereign Party). This Party was founded on 21 April 1952. After Hashim came out of jail, it was formally established in September 1953 with Hashim as its first President, and called for the formation of the anti-Muslim League United Front.[97] The party aimed at 'the realization of Islamic society in Pakistan free of all types of exploitation and tyranny'.

However, Mafidul Hoque writes that Hashim stuck to his strong anti-Communist stand,[98] and despite his call, remained outside the United Front which was formed in November 1953 to fight against the Muslim League in the election for the East Bengal Legislative Assembly to be held in March 1954. The United Front was comprised of the Awami Muslim League led by H.S. Suhrawardy, the Krishak Sramik Party led by Fazlul Huq, the Nizam-e-Islam led by Maulana Atahar Ali and the Ganatantri Dal led by Haji Mohammad Danesh.[99] For tactical reasons, the Communists did not campaign under their party banner, but preferred to contest seats as the nominees of the United Front.[100] One of the main themes in Hashim's book, *The Creed of Islam* is a critical review of 'Nihilistic Materialism'. Hashim wrote that 'Nihilistic Materialism' was not the creation of the proletariat, but was the historical development of the materialistic philosophy of life of the capitalists and their machine civilization, and added:[101]

> The world will gain nothing but stronger fetters if there is merely a change from the Imperialism and Capitalism of the Bourgeoisie to the Imperialism and centralized Capitalism of the proletariat. Materialism of the Bourgeoisie capitalism is the root and the Nihilistic Materialism of the proletariat Socialism is the fruit. The fruit shall be inevitable so long as the root is there. Therefore, the root or the mental attitude and the social order of the bourgeoisie materialism must be destroyed. For, its destruction will alone end all the ills and miseries of the world. If the root is cut the fruit will not be there.

In 1953, on the eve of the first free election which decided the destiny of the people in East Bengal, Abul Hashim returned to his 'principled' stance. There was no room for the logic of the 'principle of political warfare' which Hashim once taught to young Muslim League workers before the Partition.[102] In the election, the United Front won 223 seats in a House of 309, but the ruling Muslim League captured only 9 seats. The Chief Minister Nurul Amin was defeated.

The Communists won 15 seats. The result was a sweeping victory for the United Front. However, the Khilafat-e-Rabbani Party, which fought alone, got miserable results, and won only one seat. Abul Hashim, who stood from the Old Dhaka constituency, was defeated, and even lost his security deposit.[103] Later, he was unsatisfied with the behaviour of the members of his party, and left it silently in 1956. Hashim writes in his autobiography that he joined the Muslim League in 1956, though, in fact, he was politically inactive.[104]

Anwar Dil and Afia Dil write about Hashim's activities after his migration to Dhaka as follows:[105]

> Abul Hashim did not have deep ties in East Bengal and in the new political climate with his erstwhile political opponents all at the helm of affairs he found himself totally isolated. He was only approached when his name could add dignity to an undertaking, for example, to the cause of the Bengal Language Movement which was gaining momentum at the time.

However, his isolation from the mass and absorption in his Islamic studies had already started before the Partition. This became fatal at the peak of the national upsurge in East Bengal, though Hashim's strong attachment to the Bangla language and culture was always there in his life. The loss of his eyesight may have also affected his political judgment in the critical period after the middle of the 1950s.[106] It is an irony of history that Ayub Khan's regime, which started 'the political dominance of the civil-military bureaucracies under the total West Pakistani control' [107] after the coup of 1958, tried to utilize Hashim's idea of Islam, on which people made their judgment in the election of 1954.

V

On 17 April 1959 the Pakistan government under Ayub Khan took over Progressive Papers Limited which was publishing the *Pakistan Times* and *Imroze*.[108] Its owner was Mian Iftikhar-ud-din who had been critical of political process in Pakistan after her independence. He was also a leading figure of the 'Progressives' or the Left in the Punjab during the Pakistan movement. He passed away on 6 June 1962, but till his death he fought against the Martial Law regime.

In March of the same year Hashim met Ayub Khan in Karachi. The meeting was extended for more than three hours. Originally it was set for only fifteen minutes.[109] Who and which side made the first approach is not yet so clear. But, from this meeting the most tragic drama was destined for the latest years of his political life. Despite the warning from his surrounding people, Hashim saw in the Ayub regime a peerless chance to realise the Islamic way of life in Pakistan which he had so far dreamed, while Ayub saw in the thought of Abul Hashim a most effective ideological means to control the upsurge of Bangla nationalism under the name of Islam. In fact, there was an ideological base which was ready to accept Ayub's dictatorship in his theory of the political leadership which appeared in his book, *The Creed of Islam*.[110]

We can notice the continuity of this theory in his book which was published in 1965 in the midst of the Ayub's regime:[111]

Social democracy in Islam means just and equitable distribution of rights and privileges of society and state. Any social superstructure in a given society suitable for implementing this democracy is Islamic. The spirit is eternal, but the form of social machinery necessary for implementing the spirit of democracy changes with varying material conditions of existence. To hold fast to the outer form in colossal ignorance of the spirit is un-Islamic. Fundamentals of Islamic social order were as perfectly implemented by the faithful Caliphs of Islam as they could be in the context of the then prevailing conditions of life.

The relationship of mutual trust between Ayub Khan and Abul Hashim, established in the meeting, was changeless till Ayub's regime was removed, and Hashim also tried to perform his duty sincerely in his own way as a 'humble thinker who tries to think in concrete terms'.[112] Because of this sincerity the scale of the tragedy was immeasurable.

The result of the meeting soon appeared in the limelight for the 'humble thinker' who felt isolated from the erstwhile opponents, comrades and sympathizers in his political struggle after his migration to Dhaka in 1950. Even in the language movement of 1952, he joined it as a private person.

In October 1960 the Government reorganized the Darul Ulm in Dhaka as the Islamic Academy, and on 8 November, Abul Hashim was appointed as its first Director, and remained in this post till the middle of 1970.[113] The translation of the Quran into Bangla was one of the main results in the Academy. Hashim was the Chairman of the Board of Translators.[114] In the symposiums, while severely criticizing the materialism in the West, Abul Hashim tried to keep his rational attitudes in his interpretation of Islam, rejecting emotional stance.[115]

Despite his devoted work in the Academy it is difficult to reject the following conclusion expressed by Mafidul Hoque (translated by Kuwajima).[116]

> Side by side it must be admitted that, behind the foundation of the Islamic Academy the selfish intention of the ruling class in Pakistan was working, namely the utilization of Islam for the purpose of strengthening the system of their rule and exploitation. The Islamic Academy played this role too.
>
> And, while he was engaged in the work of the Islamic Academy, his social isolation became deeper. When the political upheaval in the entire East Bengal gradually advanced towards its final stage, and the people were agitated by the development of the national consciousness, we can not observe its reflection in Abul Hashim. When fissure appeared in the thought of so-called

integration of Pakistan, he published a booklet, *The Integration of Pakistan*, immediately after the people's revolt of 1969. Its Bangla translation is *Pakistaner Sanhoti*.

Simultaneously Mafidul Hoque appreciated that the influence of Hashim's attachment to Bangla language was clearly noticed in the publications of the Islamic Academy. Also, on 5 July 1968 Abul Hashim criticized the behaviour of those people who 'defended the removal of Rabindranath Sangeeta under the name of the ideal of Islam and Pakistan'. In the end of 1969, Abul Hashim joined the movement against the ban on many publications by the Pakistan Government.[117]

However, the shadow of the Ayub regime on the political life of Abul Hashim was obvious. In August 1962 Hashim was appointed a member of the Islamic Ideology Council of Pakistan, and also became the Chief Organizer, East Pakistan Muslim League, Ayub Khan's so called Convention Muslim League in September 1962. These were the legal and political machineries in accordance with the new Constitution promulgated on 1 March 1962. Under this system, Ayub Khan did not hesitate to meet Maulana Bhashani, a peasant leader and a leading figure of the National Awami Party in East Pakistan. The meeting was held in Rawalpindi on 22 August 1963 at the invitation of Ayub.[118] There was considerable conjecture as to the meaning of the meeting.

Earlier, Suhrawardy, who had come out of jail on 19 August 1962, declared the formation of the National Democratic Front. The 'democratization of the Constitution' was its main slogan.[119] Bhashani, who became free on 3 November 1962, joined the Front. On the other hand, even Khwaja Nazimuddin, who was a leader of the Pakistan Muslim League (Council) called for the restoration of parliamentary democracy. In this connection, Badruddin Umar sarcastically expressed his observation that, in the year of 1965, in the eyes of the common people not only Shahid Suhrawardy, but even Khwaja Nazimuddin had become leftists.[120] Despite his devoted work, Abul Hashim could not perceive what was going on in the 1960s 'under the name of the ideal of Islam and Pakistan'.

In the days of the Bangladeshi war for independence he did not participate in it positively, but made no contact with the ruling class in Pakistan. Mafidul Hoque made remarks that under the circumstances no action indirectly had positive meaning to men of great personality like Hashim.[121] Mohammad Abdul Gafoor also writes that, despite strong pressure, Hashim did not issue any statement in support of the action of the Pakistani Army.[122]

After the independence of Bangladesh Abul Hashim lived almost in retirement, and breathed his last on 5 October 1974.

Conclusion

Mohammad Abdul Gafoor lamented in the above-mentioned article that Abul Hashim's birth centenary (27 January 2005) was passing off with no special respect paid to him, despite the fact that he laid the basis of Bangladesh in his ideas expressed in his approach to the Lahore Resolution of 1940, and that his followers secured positions of power after her independence.

Hasan Zaheer, who first served in East Pakistan till 1962, and finally as the deputy commissioner to Jessore before his return to West Pakistan, was later posted in Dhaka in May 1971, and found that he 'was not regarded as one of them, or for them'.[123] Though he did not mention the latest activities of Abul Hashim, he remarked that Hashim, in his earlier days, was 'a secular Bengali nationalist, who enjoyed the support of students and was greatly influenced by communist ideology and organizational techniques'.[124] Gafoor also emphasizes that, unlike other leaders in the Pakistan movement, Abul Hashim's view was not communal, but that Hashim thought that India consisted of not one nation or two nations, but multi-nations. In this respect Abul Hashim found in the Lahore Resolution the political basis of his idea, and had also something in common with the political approach of the Communist Party of India during the 'People's War' period of 1942–45, which admitted the right of self-determination of each 'nationality'. It is generally admitted among those reviewers who appreciate Hashim's idea positively that he was a dynamic League leader during this period, and stimulated the idea of young educated Bengali Muslims who fought against the vested interests in the Bengal League represented by the Khwaja and the Ispahani. The thought and activities of Hashim contributed to the growth of the Bengal Muslim League as a mass organization. His ideas included a message to the Bengal Muslims whom the Indian National Congress and other political organizations had so far failed to organize on a full scale.

However, Baddruddin Umar questions the meaning of the Lahore Resolution from the standpoint of the minority problem.[125] Unlike Abul Hashim, Umar did not find any difference between the partition of India and that of Bengal and the Punjab.

> The partition of India, Bengal and the Punjab in 1947 instead of solving the religious minority problem, which was its ostensible objective, in fact consolidated much more firmly the rule of religious majorities in what previously constituted British India.
>
> There was nothing surprising in this, because the 1940 Lahore Resolution of the Muslim League proposed to create separate states in the Muslim majority areas of east and west India. Thus, in real terms, there was no question of solving the religious minority problems in India either for the Muslims or for the Hindus and other peoples in the declared objectives of either the Congress or the Muslim League.

In Umar's analysis this was the result of the stance of the Indian feudal-bourgeois classes, belonging to the Hindu and Muslim majority community respectively, who tried to consolidate their interests. This critical view demands a re-examination of even the main ideological basis of Hashim's idea.

As we noted earlier, Nikhil Chakravarty mentioned, as one of the reasons of the growth of the Bengal League, the terrible experience of the famine which, along with 'a timid role' of the League Ministry to tackle the problem, convinced the younger generation of Muslims that the only way to make the League strong was to go out among the people. However, there is a dearth of sources in the form of recollections or researches to prove how young League workers had critical views of the food policy of the League Ministry or went out 'among the people' who were struggling with the famine, and extended their relief activities, though there are some documents to show that these activists and workers were very active in their appeal to the people in their election campaigns. As for the communist relief activities, we can find some important literature[126], and, a communist, who was critical of the official policy of the Communist Party of India in 1942–47, appreciates the 'dedicated relief work for the victims of the famine in and after 1943' extended by the Communists.[127] The largest victims in the famine of 1943 were agricultural labourers, belonging to the Hindu, Muslim, and other weaker sections. Also, as for the victims in the Hindu-Muslim riots in the 1940s, Amartya Sen writes, on the basis of his own observation of a victimized Muslim unemployed labourer in 1944, that, even though the community identity of the exterminated preys was quite different, their class identities were often extremely similar.[128]

How did the Progressives or the Left of the Bengal Muslim League connect their minority-majority consciousness with their approach to the imminent critical situation which the people of Bengal, and the lowest classes in particular faced? In this respect, we are still at the starting point of the study on Abul Hashim, though there are many words lavishly showered on his ideas and activities in 1943–45.

In the 1960s, Abul Hashim became a part of the Ayub regime, while his erstwhile followers played a prominent part in the movement of Bangladesh for self-government and independence. In his last days, Hashim also tried to express something by his silence. However, the movement for independence in the last stage took the form of the people's movement which Hashim felt it difficult to realize in his earlier days. It may be said that, though Hashim became sidelined from the main stream of politics after 1947 except the year 1952, his earlier idea remained functioning. It is not accidental that, though he was expected to play his role as a part of the Ayub regime, particularly in the field of his Islamic thought, Abul Hashim's contribution in this period was rather observed in his activities which reflected his attachment to Bengali culture. This contribution was brought out not only by his idea but the emerging political climate which existed as a strong undercurrent. However, we cannot deny the fact that Ayub Khan and Hashim caused resonance with each other in their thoughts on Islam and critical views of the political leaders in Pakistan, in spite of whatever differences they may have had in their basic approach to Islam and the society. It was this discrepancy between Hashim's idea and the people's movement, and between his conviction as a scholar of Islam and the earnest aspiration of the people in Bengal that brought to light the tragic role of Abul Hashim under the Ayub regime.

While the loss of his eyesight cultivated his strong will to challenge even established leaders in the past, he failed to see political intrigues in the critical moment.

What is to be examined is whether or not there was a bud in his dynamic thoughts and actions in 1943–45 which led to his later tragic role in the 1960s. Inversely, even in his tragic days, there were positive aspects in his thoughts and actions which could be traced to his earlier days. When Hashim was a 'secular Bengali nationalist', it was in the days when he was attracted to the idea of 'Rabbaniyat'. His activities in the Tamaddun Majlish, an Islamic organization, led him to join the language movement in 1952. And, when he shared Ayub's idea of 'Islamic' policy, he demonstrated his attachment to the language and culture of Bengal. His philosophy of 'Rabbaniyat', and his theory of multi-nationalism and non-communalism may explain his political action in certain stages of his life. However, there was some ambiguity in his ideas, which acted positively or negatively according to the situation. What is to be noted is how the aspirations of people in South Asia of the 1940s drove Hashim to action, and how Hashim responded to this demand of the times. His idea and work in the 1940s molded the basic framework of his political thought, though other factors also contributed to its later development and deviation. The examination of the ideas and works of Abul Hashim in the long term perspective and the re-examination of the terminology which is used to express the particular aspects of his thoughts, leads us to the well-balanced appreciation of his earlier political life, which tried to be free from 'communalism' while he considered Islam as the source for political and social change.

Endnotes

1 Sho Kuwajima, 'Mian Iftikhar-ud-Din (1907–1962)—"National Self-Determination" and a Contemporary History of Pakistan—' (in Japanese), *Journal of Osaka University of Foreign Studies*, No. 55, 1982, pp. 13–34.

2 Sho Kuwajima, 'A Democrat in Pakistan, *Pakistan: The First Twelve Years: The Pakistan Times: Editorials of Mazhar Ali Khan*, Oxford University Press, Karachi', *Biblio: A Review of Books*, New Delhi, December 1997, pp. 13–4.

3 Abul Hashim. 1974. *In Retrospection*, Dhaka: Subarna Publishers.

4 Mafidul Hoque. 1990. *Abul Hashim 1905–1974* (in Bangla), Dhaka: Bangla Academy and Syed Mansur Ahmad, 'Abul Hashim: Bangali Musalman', in Syed Mansur Ahmad (ed.). 2000. *Abul Hashim-Tanr Jiban o Samaya*(in Bangla), Dhaka: Jatyo Grantha Prakashan.
5 Kamruddin Ahmad. 1382 (Bengal Calendar). *Banglar Madyavitter Atmavikash* (in Bangla), Vol. 2, Dhaka: Zahiruddin Mahmud Inside Library.
6 Harun-or-Rashid. 2003. *The Foreshadowing of Bangladesh-Bengal Muslim League and Muslim Politics 1906–1947*, Revised and enlarged edition, Dhaka: The University Press.
7 Sho Kuwajima. 1998. *Muslims, Nationalism and the Partition—1946 Provincial Elections in India*, New Delhi: Manohar Publishers & Distributors.
8 Hashim, op. cit., p. 30.
9 ibid., pp. 31–2. At the First Indian Communist Conference in Kanpur (26–28 December 1925), Azad Subhani was selected as a member of the Central Executive, and also as its vice-president for the coming year (G. Adhikari (ed.). 1974. *Documents of the History of the Communist Party of India, Vol. 2, 1923–1925*, New Delhi: People's Publishing House, p. 667). The process of later metamorphosis of his idea is not clear.
10 Hoque, op. cit., p. 37.
11 Hashim, op. cit., p. 1.
12 ibid., p. 3.
13 Syed Mansur Ahmad, op. cit., p. 426.
14 Hashim, op. cit., pp. 15–6.
15 Joya Chatterji. 1995. *Bengal Divided-Hindu Communalism and Partition, 1932–1947*, New Delhi: Foundation Books, pp. 213–14. By the way, after the May 2006 Assembly elections and the victory of the Left Front in West Bengal, *the Frontline* described Burdwan as 'the rice bowl and Left bastion of West Bengal' in its issue of 2 June 2006, p. 10.
16 Hashim, op. cit., 17–8.
17 ibid., pp. 22–3.
18 Syed Mansur Ahmad, op. cit., p. 424 and pp. 428–9.
19 Hashim, op. cit., p. 20.
20 Hoque, op. cit., pp. 31–2.
21 Hashim, op. cit., pp. 52–3.
22 Kamruddin Ahmad, op. cit., pp. 22–3.
23 As for Maulana Akram Khan, see Amalendu De. 1996. *Religious Fundamentalism and Secularism in India*, Baharampur (West Bengal): Suryasena Prakashani, p. 85.
24 Kamruddin Ahmad, op. cit., p. 21. This part is also cited by Anwar Dil and Afia Dil. 2000. *Bengali Language Movement to Bangladesh*, San Diego and Islamabad: Intercultural Forum, p. 287.

25 Kamruddin Ahmad, op. cit., pp. 24–6.
26 Hashim, op. cit., p. 70.
27 Harun-or-Rashid, op. cit., p. 155.
28 ibid., pp. 159–60.
29 Hashim, op. cit., pp. 57–8.
30 ibid., p. 72.
31 *People's War*, 3 December 1944.
32 Hoque, op. cit., p. 46.
33 Hashim, op. cit., p. 33.
34 Harun-or-Rashid, op. cit., p. 162.
35 Hashim, op. cit., pp. 77–8.
36 Harun-or-Rashid, op. cit., p. 162.
37 Hashim, op. cit., p. 79.
38 *People's War*, 15 April 1945.
39 Hashim, op. cit., pp. 79–80. Also see, Harun-or-Rashid, op. cit., p. 164.
40 Hashim, op. cit., p. 82.
41 Hoque, op. cit., p. 55.
42 ibid., p. 48.
43 Hashim, op. cit., pp. 171–2.
44 For details, see Kuwajima, *Muslims, Nationalism and the Partition*, pp. 54–6.
45 Harun-or-Rashid, op. cit., p. 185.
46 *People's War*, 28 August 1945.
47 Harun-or-Rashid, op. cit., pp. 233–4.
48 Hashim, op. cit., p. 109.
49 ibid., pp. 109–10, and Kamruddin Ahmad. 1970. *A Social History of Bengal*, Dhaka: Raushan Ara Ahmad, 3rd edition, pp. 68–9.
50 Kamruddin Ahmad, *Social History*, p. 69.
51 Harun-or-Rashid, op. cit., pp. 236–9.
52 Hashim, op. cit., p. 110.
53 *Dawn*, 10 April 1946.
54 Hoque, op. cit., pp. 61–2.
55 Kamruddin Ahmad, *Atmavikash*, pp. 69–70.
In this meeting attended following leaders; Shamsuddin Ahmad (Kushtiyar), Kamruddin Ahmad, Shamsul Huq, Shamsuddin Ahmad (Dhaka), Nuruddin Ahmad, Nurul Alam, Sheikh Mujibur Rahman, Mohammad Toaha, and Khondkar Mushtaq Ahmad (Badruddin Umar. 2004. *Amar Jivan 1 (1931–1950)*, Dhaka: Sahittika, pp. 154–5).
56 Kamruddin Ahmad, *Social History*, pp. 75–6.
57 Abul Mansur Ahmad. 1978. *Atmakatha* (in Bangla), Dhaka: Mohiuddin Ahmad, pp. 222–3.
Abul Mansur Ahmad drafted the 21–point programme adopted by the United Front in November 1953 on the occasion of the general election to the East Bengal Legislative Assembly, Kamal Uddin

Ahmad, "1954 Elections: Issues of Autonomy", in Sirajul Islam (ed.). 1992. *History of Bangladesh 1704–1971, Vol. 1, Political History*, Dhaka: Asiatic Society of Bangladesh, p. 465.

58 Kamruddin Ahmad, *Social History*, p. 76.

59 Harun-or-Rashid, op. cit., p. 249.

60 Hashim, op. cit., pp. 131–2.

61 ibid., p. 131, and Harun-or-Rashid, op. cit., pp. 249–53.

62 Hoque, op. cit., p. 76.

63 Kamruddin Ahmad, *Atmavikash*, p. 81. Also see Hoque, op. cit., p. 76.

64 Kamruddin Ahmad, *Social History*, p. 76.

65 Hoque, op. cit., pp. 76–7.

66 Harun-or-Rashid, op. cit., pp. 257–322. Also see Harun-or-Rashid, "A Move for United Independent Bengal", in Sirajul Islam (ed.), op. cit., pp. 400–21, and Amalendu De. 2003. *Swadhin Bangabhumi Gathaner Parikalpana-Prayash o Parinati* (in Bangla), 2nd edition, Agartala: Parul Prakashani.

67 Harun-or-Rashid, *Foreshadowing*, p. 258.

68 De, *Swadhin Bangabhumi*, pp. 39–43.

69 Hashim, op. cit., pp. 139–43.

70 De, *Swadhin Bangabhumi*, op. cit., p. 98.

71 Harun-or-Rashid, *Foreshadowing*, pp. 294–5.

72 De, *Swadhin Bangabhumi*, pp. 45–55.

73 Harun-or-Rashid, *Foreshadowing*, p. 277 and p. 313.

74 ibid., p. 316.

75 ibid.

76 ibid., p. 320.

77 Hashim, op. cit., pp. 159–60.

78 *Dawn*, 14 June 1947.

79 Hashim, op. cit., p. 163.

80 ibid.

81 ibid., pp. 163–4.

82 Syed Mansur Ahmad, op. cit., pp. 461–2.

83 Hoque, op. cit., pp. 90–1. On 12 April Badruddin Umal, Hashim's son, reached Dhaka, and, Hashim and other family members reached on 22 April. Also, see Syed Mansur Ahmad, op. cit., pp. 462–4.

84 Abul Hashim. 1985. *The Creed of Islam or the Revolutionary Character of Kalima*, 4th edition, Dhaka: Islamic Foundation Bangladesh, p. xiii.

85 ibid., p. 13.

86 ibid., p. vii.

87 ibid., p. vii and p. viii.

88 ibid., pp. 99–101. Also, see Hoque, op. cit., p. 98.

89 Hoque, op. cit., p. 91.

90 ibid., p. 92, and Mohammad Abdul Gafoor, "Nishabde Atikrant hoe gel Darshanik—Rajnitivid Allama Abul Hashimer Janma Shatavarshiki", *Dainik Inkilab*(in Bangla), 26 January 2005.
91 Badruddin Umar, "Language Movement", in Sirajul Islam (ed.), op. cit., p. 424.
92 ibid., p. 447.
93 ibid., p. 448.
94 ibid., p. 449.
95 ibid., pp. 449–50.
96 ibid., p. 457.
97 M. B. Nair. 1990. *Politics in Bangladesh—A Study of Awami League 1949–58*, New Delhi: Northern Book Centre and Hoque, op. cit., p. 94.
98 ibid., pp. 94–5.
99 Kamal Uddin Ahmed, op. cit., p. 464.
100 ibid., p. 472.
101 Hashim, *Creed of Islam*, pp. 126–7.
102 Hashim, *In Retrospection*, p. 59.
103 Hoque, op. cit., p. 95.
104 ibid.
105 Anwar Dil and Afia Dil, op. cit., p. 292.
106 Syed Mansur Ahmad, op. cit., p. 469.
107 Harun-or-Rashid, *Foreshadowing*, p. 339.
108 Tariq Ali. 1970. *Pakistan—Military Rule or People's Power*, New York: William Morrow and Company, pp. 101–4.
109 Hoque, op. cit., p. 96.
110 ibid., p. 98.
111 Abul Hashim. 1980. *As I See It*, 2nd edition, Dhaka: Islamic Foundation, Bangladesh, p. 22.
112 ibid., Author's Preface.
113 Hoque, op. cit., p. 100 and p. 106.
114 ibid., p. 104.
115 ibid., pp. 101–4.
116 ibid., p. 105.
117 ibid., pp. 105–6.
118 Saiyid Abul Maksud. 1994. *Maulana Abdul Hamid Khan Bhashani* (in Bangla), Dhaka: Bangla Academy Dhaka, p. 244.
119 ibid., p. 241.
120 Hoque, op. cit., p. 113.
121 ibid., p. 111.
122 Gafoor, op. cit.
123 Hasan Zaheer. 1994. *The Separation of East Pakistan—The Rise and Realization of Bengali Muslim Nationalism*, Dhaka: University Press Limited, p. xv.
124 ibid., p. 8.

125 Badruddin Umar, 'Class struggles in East Pakistan and the emergence of Bangladesh-Pakistan and the minority question', *Holiday*, 14 August, 1998.

126 Saroj Mukhopadhyay. 1986. *Bharater Communist Party o Amara* (in Bangla), Kolkata: National Book Agency.

127 Arindam Sen, 'Indian Communists in Freedom Movement: Yesterday and Today', *Liberation-Central Organ of CPI(ML)*, October 2005.

128 Amartya Sen. 2005. *The Argumentative Indian-Writing on Indian History, Culture and Identity*, London: Allen Lane, p. 209.

Notes

My interest in the thought of Abul Hashim started in the middle of the 1960s. However, this is still an interim report due to my laziness and failure in finding out some of the primary sources.

In preparing this paper I owe much to the help and co-operation extended to me by my friends for a long time.

I would like to express my grateful thanks to Professor K.M. Mohsin, who kindly helped my work in various ways since 1978, and provided me some important literature in connection with the life of Abul Hashim. Also, I am thankful for the help by Professor Harun-or-Rashid, who kindly found out some works written by Abul Hashim.

I also would like to express my thanks to Professor Amalendu De, who also provided me many useful sources on Hashim studies.

On the occasion of my visit to Dhaka in August 2007, I could get some recent books and precious information from Mr. Badruddin Umar. As most of this manuscript was prepared in 2006, here I could use them only partially. I would like to revise and enlarge it in near future.

It is no need of saying that only I am responsible for the view expressed here.

6

Post Script: Recollecting my Sapru House Days 1962–66

Sho Kuwajima

I

I joined the Indian School of International Studies, a predecessor of Jawaharlal Nehru University, in October 1962 under the Government of India Scholarships Scheme. This school, which started at Sapru House, New Delhi in 1955, was a product of the Asian Relations Conference held in New Delhi from March to April 1947, and played pioneering part in both International Studies and Area Studies in India.

As a small autonomous institution, it had no student hostel at that time. Though I stayed at the International Students House, which was provisionally located at Timar Pur near Delhi University, the room was not suitable for research work. After I had made contact with various organizations including the Ministry of Education, finally in September 1963, special arrangement was made for my stay in a room of Gwyer Hall, Delhi University by an agreement between Dr. A. Appadolai, Director of the School, and the Vice-Chancellor, Delhi University. In Gwyer Hall, I enjoyed quiet hostel life. I remember a peaceful Diwali festival of 1963 decorated with small candles on the doorsteps of employees' quarters, and without the noise of crackers.

After one year, I had to leave the Hall rather unceremoniously, most probably due to my refusal to respond to the personal request of a clerk. On that occasion he spoke to me quite smilingly. But, after one or two days when I was called again to his office, I was told bluntly that I should leave the Hall immediately as the newly built International Students House had started functioning on the Mall Road. I left Gwyer Hall partly reluctantly, but partly willingly. In the new House, a student from Nepal, Komal Bahadur Chitrakar, with whom I had shared a room for about five months in my Timar Pur days, and later a public accountant, Jaswant Singh, a bearer and Kilu Ram, a sweeper whose nice service I had got there, were ready to welcome my coming back. Moreover, a few months before, when I was looking at the peacocks inside the Hall, I was suddenly attacked on my back by a big monkey. Since then I developed a 'monkey-phobia'. When monkeys were freely moving in the corridor in front of my room, or on the back verandah, I was forced to stay in the room as if I was behind the iron bars of a jail. I felt relief when I left Gwyer Hall, though I missed its quiet atmosphere. I could make many new friends in the new International Students House, and one of them, Mr. P.C. Singla, later a public accountant, was a life long friend. Hostel life together with Mr. K.B. Chitrakar led me to my interest in the contemporary history of Nepal.

I went to the Indian School of International Studies for three years, taking bus from Mall Road to Mandi House or the Modern School. Going by bus every day was tough work. It took time for me to catch a bus, though I learnt patience. However, the scenery of Delhi from the Old Secretariat, Kashmiri Gate, Lal Quila, Darya Ganj to Barakhamba Road, and the life of the people observed from a bus window, was an important and enjoyable source of my study. The beautifully decorated show window of a small bookshop, Raj Pal & Sons, always attracted my attention. Later in 1975,

I visited the shop in search of a recent reprint of the biography of Mazzini written in Hindi or Urdu by Lala Lajpat Rai. The shopkeeper brought from a back room *Mahatma Gwisep Mezzini ka Jivan Charitra* (A Life of Mazzini) translated into Hindi from Urdu and published in 1921. He did not demand a special price for this book. I felt something deeply cultured in his simple attitude. In the bus I could meet a well-known scholar unexpectedly, and a pickpocket too. The bus was truly the place to learn about the people and society of India, and actually it was on the window frame of a bus that I learnt a full sentence in Hindi for the first time. It was *Shikayat ki Kitab Conductor ke pas hai* (a complaint book is available in the hands of a conductor).

I still remember one of the unforgettable scenes when I stayed at the new International Students House. Under the heavy monsoon rain there was no bus service, though I had an important appointment at the school. Hearing my difficulty, a shoe polisher handed me five Rupees, advising me to go by auto-rickshaw. I declined to receive it, thanking for his sympathy. In 1975, when I visited the International Students House again, the employees welcomed me with chai and tobacco.

By the way, near Kashmiri Gate I always noticed a big standing signboard from the window of a bus. On this board, a picture of the Prime Minister Nehru was painted with his call, 'We welcome foreigners as our guests'. This is a rather formal expression. During my stay in India, I had many 'informal' experiences, which could not be simply classified as experiences as 'foreign guests'.

In this connection, the recollection of Dr. S. Seshaiah who made a field survey in a village in North-Eastern Japan, and analysed the results of the land reform conducted after the Second World War, attracts our attention.[1] It discloses delicate relations between the Japanese, who received a foreigner politely, but with some distance of mind, and a foreign scholar who wanted to know Japan and the Japanese 'from within':

I arrived at the village in August 1961, and stayed with a farmer's household as a *'geshuku'* (paying guest). As a foreigner, I was a privileged person. When I wanted to meet anyone in the village, there was no need to introduce myself; villagers had come to know my stay and the purpose of my stay, without my telling everyone. Yet, it was not an unmixed blessing. While I found it easy to elicit information on facts and figures, when discussion touched on interpersonal and inter-group relations, the villagers did not seem to share their thoughts freely with me. When discussion touched on *specific* interpersonal relations such as, for example, the strained relations between landlord A and tenant B, there seemed to be greater restraint. The response to such specific relations when it involved them directly would usually evoke 'condensed' answers in the form of *"hitoguchi de ieba"* (to say it in one word), which were suggestive but not detailed. This restricted me to some extent in understanding the social change 'from within' in terms of their own values and meanings. Although I lived amidst them, ate their food, and even donned *'yukata'*, I remained an outsider. I was welcomed and given access to all village documents, and was provided with information willingly on matters which did not concern them directly, again as a privileged foreigner. But, I must confess that I remained as a happier position as a privileged foreigner.

Dr. Seshaiah encountered Japanese society where the villagers did not want to expose internal conflicts to the 'outsiders'. This was not only his problem, but perhaps many Indians also faced the same type of problem when they wanted to live in Japan as a member of the society or the area.

II

I left Yokohama on 22 September, and reached Bombay by sea on 10 October 1962. Bombay Port was in the midst of a labour strike, and the ship could not come alongside the quay. Though I already had the knowledge of the Royal

Indian Navy strike in Bombay, February 1946 as a part of the freedom struggle in India, I never expected the 'welcome' labour strike. I had to reach the quay alone by a small boat. I felt a great relief when I found Mr. Gulati of Indian Council of Cultural Relations (ICCR) who had been waiting long to receive me. I reached Delhi by train on 14 October, and joined the school next day. On the 16th, on the occasion of the first lecture on International Politics, Dr. Appadolai said that the Japanese language was very difficult, and therefore Japanese academic results did not reach outside. He was happy to find that I had joined the school. 'We can know from you what the Japanese are thinking of.'

However, on 20 October, 'India China War', or 'Sino-Indian Conflicts' started. The news on the 'Chinese Aggression' prevailed in every corner of the city. I was so often mistaken as a Chinese in the bus or in the streets. I felt it a bit difficult to adjust myself to the heated discussion among the staff and students of the school. The lack of proper accommodation was at the bottom of my unrest.

During the summer vacation from the middle of May to the middle of July 1963, I stayed at the Guest House of the Bhandharkar Oriental Research Institute, Poona, with the kind arrangement of Dr. Nakada Naomichi, who was once working at this institute. I needed rest, and therefore two months in Poona became a very refreshing experience. Besides going to the Library of the Gokhale Institute of Politics and Economics, I enjoyed observing the active life of the people in Deccan Gymkhana, Laxmi Road, and other places. Here, too, I liked the scenery observed from a bus window. I also liked the strong cool wind in the evening and *masala dosa* served at the Poona Coffee House. However, what was most stimulating were the talks with Professor D.D. Kosambi whose residence was located near the Institute. I visited there during teatime once or twice a week. Professor Kosambi kindly spared time for me till he would hear someone open the gate, and asked 'Kanu (Who)?' I learnt from him the importance of thinking independently as well as many problems of historical studies. I visited his residence again in 1964 and 1965. In January 1966 he kindly came to see me in New Delhi while I was in Bihar. Knowing that I had lost all my belongings during my trip on the Gaya-Patna passenger train, he sent me money from Poona. He earlier wrote to me, 'If you will let me know how much money will be needed to replace the clothes etc. lost, I shall send you whatever I can. I hope that you will not feel insulted at this offer, but if some countryman of mine has played so dirty a trick upon you, I can only try to redress the wrong' (8 February 1966). It was 3 months before he passed away.

By the way, my trip to Satara and Aundh was also arranged by a senior research student who once studied at the ISIS and was then living in Poona. I visited Aundh in 1964 and 1965, and could meet his old parents. Satara had been in my mind since I read Kosambi's critical reference to the Communist view of the peasant uprising in Satara of 1942–45.[2]

When I returned to Delhi in July 1963, I was very happy. First, the problem of my accommodation was solved. A batch of research scholars who joined the school in October 1962 heartily welcomed my return to Delhi, and made me quite comfortable. Among them were Dr. J.A. Naik and Dr. S. Nagarajan. I met Naik later in Kolhapur in 1989. Kolhapur reminded me of the role of the Maharaja of Kolhapur in the Non-Brahmin movement, and the disorderly session of the Indian National Congress in Surat in 1907 where Kolhapuri *chappals* were thrown. I also visited Thanjavur in 1989 where Nagarajan was working. Most probably in 1965, Nagarajan advised me to meet C. Rajagopalachari on the occasion of my visit to Madras. I wrote a letter, and got his reply. Though I can't find the original letter, the gist of his letter was 'As I am 86 years old and a tired man, I can't meet you. I advise you to meet Pyarelal.' My knowledge about Rajaji in those days, was as a proposer of the so called C.R. Formula for the solution of the Pakistan issue, the only Indian who became the Governor-General of India, and a leader of the Swatantra Party. I knew later his amazingly deep thought on India after Swaraj from his jail diary written in Vellore Jail on 24 January 1922:[3]

We all ought to know that Swaraj will not at once or, I think, even for a long time to come, be better government or greater happiness for the people. Elections and their corruptions, injustice, and the power and tyranny of wealth, and inefficiency of administration, will make a hell of life as soon as freedom is given to us. Men will look regretfully back to the old regime of comparative justice, and efficient, peaceful, more or less honest administration. The only thing gained will be that as a race we will be saved from dishonor and subordination. Hope lies only in universal education by which right conduct, fear of god, and love, will be developed among the citizens from childhood. It is only if we succeed in this that Swaraj will mean happiness. Otherwise it will mean the grinding injustices and tyranny of wealth. What a beautiful world it would be, if everybody were just and God-fearing and realized the happiness of loving other! Yet, there is more practical hope for the ultimate consummation of this ideal in India than elsewhere.

In July 1963, what made me very relaxed was that H.G. Pant, my close colleague, informed me that Dr. K.P. Karunakaran was glad to have me as his student. As I knew that the relation between supervisor and research scholar was one of the most important factors for fruitful student life in India, I was very happy to hear it. Actually Dr. Karunakaran was very generous in his guidance, and allowed me to conduct my work in my own way. Though he left the school later, and had some difficult time too, I tried to keep regular contact with him. In his latest 13 years he spent his life in a village of Kerala. When I met him in

Kochi, I found in him a very considerate intellectual who did not lose broad outlook.

When I met H.G. Pant first in October 1962, he asked, 'Do you know Takahashi?' Pant had known the name of K. Takahashi as a Japanese historian who joined the discussion about *the transition from Feudalism to Capitalism* with Maurice Dobb and Paul Sweezy. Since then in both Delhi and Jaipur we have discussed many matters concerning Indian politics, history and even literature too. When he was in Jaipur, he introduced me to Mr. Radhavallabh Agrawal, a peasant movement leader in Jaipur State. I had a chance to learn the character of the peasant movement in the princely states. The last work of Pant, a political scientist, was *Upanyas* (novel) in Hindi titled *Mritunjaya* in which he started the novel with his idea of life and death, and described the political activities of young activists.[4]

III

When I visited some parts of India, the staff and colleagues of the Indian School of International Studies, and the hostel mates of the Gwyer Hall mentioned some persons who could guide me during my trips.

From the end of 1963 to the beginning of 1964 I planned my trip to Chandigarh and Punjab. Dr. H.S. Chopra introduced me to his friend in Chandigarh. He and his mother, who were leading a modest life there, took care of me very well, and made me comfortable in their apartment. He also responded to my wish to see a village in Punjab, suggesting the Khadi Gram Udyog (Cotton Cloth Village Industries) at Adampur near Jalandhar. I enjoyed my stay at Adampur for a few days, and my visit to a neighboring village. This pleasant stay in Chandigarh and their nice care led me to a longer stay there in 1977-78. On this occasion, I could meet Principal Chabbil Das, Punjab National College at Jalandhar.[5] His talk on Bhagat Singh, a revolutionary and his student, was full of strength. I was particularly impressed by his recollection of serious discussion with Bhagat Singh, whether they should take arms for revolution, or they should deliver cheap priced literature to the people for their education. From this interview I learnt the stream of political thought from Lala Lajpat Rai to Bhagat Singh, and could make my image of the history of South Asia in the 1920s.

In May 1964, when I planned my trip to Karnataka, a hostel mate of Gwyer Hall, Dr. V.N. Subramanium, introduced me to his related person, Mr. A. Raja Rao, Staff Reporter, *Deccan Herald*. Soon after I settled into a small hotel 'room' like a birdcage, he kindly visited there, and immediately took me to his house, and entertained me with a simple but delicious vegetarian meal. Whenever I visited Bangalore, he always made me relaxed with his few words of sincerity. Also one of the staff of the ISIS suggested as my guide one young man amongst his relatives. He came to receive me at Bangalore Station. He led me not only to the various parts of Bangalore and Mysore, but also to Hassan, Belur, Halebidu and even a village near Hassan by the 3rd class coach of trains, ordinary buses and walk. While we were together, he told me frankly many problems he was facing or worrying about, for example, a serious friction between him and his father, and the difference in the way of life between his sister and her mother-in-law. In Japan, these are the family matters in which 'foreign guests' can't easily intervene, but here we exchanged our opinions freely, and shared our feeling on some parts of our lives. I was no more a foreign guest. On my return journey to Delhi in 1965, I could not get a reserved seat for the train from Mysore to Bombay. I returned to Bombay by the 3rd class coach of the express train without reservation. This was my severest train journey in India. There was no space for moving for many hours. However, this experience was rewarding.

Without my visit to Karnataka in 1964 and 1965, my interest in the modern history of Karnataka and a comparative view of the history of the Mysore Princely State and the other parts of India or the history of Japan could not have been developed.[6]

IV

I have written about my trips to Bihar in 1964, 1965, and 1966 in many places of my writings. Here, I want to avoid the repetition of my description as much as possible. [7]

My first trip to Bihar in October 1964 was also realized by the help of a colleague of the ISIS, Dr. R.C. Pradhan. In May and June of this year I met a Japanese scholar, Dr. Sugimoto Takushu from Patna who came to Poona for his work. I promised to meet him in Patna.

Till then I tried to find out the character of the Second World War by my study of the Quit India movement and the Bengal Famine of 1943. Bihar was one of the centers of the movement. I had an idea of the movement by reading K.K. Datta's *Freedom Movement in Bihar*, and other works. On the other hand, my knowledge of the history of the peasant movement, and the role of the peasants in the Quit India movement was extremely limited. Except some works on the peasant uprisings in the nineteenth century there were very few results on the peasant movement in the twentieth century India. I knew Rahul Sankrityayan as a peasant movement leader, but my knowledge of Swami Sahajanand Saraswati was through R. Coupland's *Indian Politics 1936–1942*, and Leonard Schiff's *The Present Condition of India* (Japanese translation appeared in 1942). My thirst for knowledge had not been fulfilled, though, by then, I came to find my modest life in India quite satisfactory.

In October 1964, I got down from the train at Dumraon Station. R.C. Pradhan was there to receive me, and took me to his village. He kindly guided me to the various parts of the village. I enjoyed my talk with villagers and their welcome music in the starlight. Next morning I took the train to Patna. This one day experience in the village made me feel very familiar with Bihar.

Dr. Bimal Prasad, then a visiting professor from Patna, wrote an introduction letter to the university administration and his former colleague, Professor R.S. Sharma, Department of History, Patna University. I met Professor Walter Hauser in the classroom where Professor Sharma was teaching. Professor Hauser kindly spared time for me to provide information on the peasant movement in Bihar and the life of Swami Sahajanand Saraswati. He introduced me to Dr. K.K. Datta, and also took me to the various institutions, Bihar State Archives, Secretariat Library, and Sacchhidananda Sinha Library. I still feel very sorry that he was drenched in the *hathiya* rain in the last stage of this guidance by rickshaw. In this trip to Patna I could get Swami Sahajanand Saraswati's *Mera Jivan Sangharsh,* and Rahul Sankrityayan's *Meri Jivan Yatra* –2. Through these two books I came to think of the character of the Second World War in the background of the historical development in the 1930s. What I learnt most from their description of the peasant movement in Bihar of the 1930s was the relation between leaders and peasants. Leaders led the peasants in the movement, but peasants also led leaders to action. I now came to know the possibility of historical sources written in Hindi language. It was from this belief that I could pick up many works written in Hindi in my university class continuously from 1966 to 2000, though at first it was very difficult to find proper textbooks, or get them from India. The later half of *Mera Jivan Sangharsh* was read through in the classroom, though we completed reading it just before my retirement in 2000.

The second visit to Bihar was realized in October 1965 after I completed three years of my stay in India. During a three month stay in Patna, Dr. K.K. Datta helped me a lot, providing not only facilities for my work at the Bihar State Archives, but also for my comfortable stay at the university hostels both in Patna and Gaya, though he did talk less. Mr. Tara Saran Singh, Bihar State Archives, responded to my request for proper sources nicely in this connection. Dr. V.A. Narain, Department of History, Patna University encouraged my work at the various stages of my work.

I became a good friend of Dr. Sugimoto who was staying at Hathwa Hostel. I also stayed at the same hostel for most of these three months. We went to the Sonepur *mela* (Animal Fair at Sonepur) together. Generally I took breakfast at the 'restaurant' under the tent, Law College. Without any order, the cooks and waiters brought me the same menu for breakfast. Once, when I sat at the same place of the 'restaurant' in the evening, without asking they brought me the same meal. For lunch, I took snacks and chai at the canteen of the Secretariat. As one of the Government employees commented, *sarkari chai* (tea prepared by the Government) was strong and not tasty. Occasionally I took a vegetarian *thali* at the restaurant on the platform of Patna station, and sometime at a restaurant of Mahendru Ghat facing the Ganga.

I could meet some political leaders who joined or led the Quit India movement. My diary and a notebook, which recorded my every day work and thought from November 1965 to January 1966, were among the things lost in January 1966, and therefore I can't recollect correctly how we met or who introduced me to these leaders. Basawan Singh was very helpful, though he did not talk about his own action connected with the activities of Jaya Prakash Narayan. Very often I visited his residence near the Secretariat early morning, and he quietly mentioned some persons whom I should meet.

One of them was Pandit Jadunandan Sharma. Those leaders not only provided information about their own historical experiences, but also tried to show me the society or the movement with which they were connected at that time. Ramanand Tiwary, who was well known for his leadership in the police strike at Jamshedpur during the Quit India movement, took me to the meeting of Panchayat Samiti at Bihiya. Karpoori Thakur, who led the movement in the Darbhanga district, proposed me to join their plan to visit the district for seeing the villages. He proposed this on our first meeting at his residence of the MLA (Member of Legislative Assembly) Block. In 1965 it was not so easy for us to go to Darbhanga from Patna. After a few days, I got into a boat in the evening at Mahendru Ghat. After reaching the other side of the Ganga, I ran to the station with a porter to occupy my seat for the night train journey. I reached Sakri in the morning, and from there used a rickshaw to Pandaul, and there waited the arrival of Karpooriji. As I have mentioned in many other places, what struck me in this one week trip to various parts of the present day Darbhanga and Madhuvani districts was an appeal of a middle aged landless labourer who when he refused to work under the unbearable condition, was beaten harshly by a landowner, and had to leave his wife and children on the premises of the landlord. I could not judge whether this man was crying or laughing, and it was only interrupted by a few words of Karpooriji. I felt unrest on that day as I could not understand the situation. Next day Karpooriji explained it was an appeal of a landless labourer. He confessed that he was helpless, but that this was the condition after twenty years of India's independence. After saying this, he was silent for sometime in the same rickshaw. Whenever I recollect my days with Karpooriji in Darbhanga, this scene first comes to my mind. In 1985, I could say thanks to Karpooriji for his hospitality of 1965-66. I could visit Darbhanga again in 2006 after 41 years.

On 16 January 1966, I lost all my belongings, except my passport, on the Gaya-Patna Passenger train which started at 11.56a.m. Among them were collected research materials in these two months, and a book, Swami Sahajanand Saraswati's *Kisan Sabha ke Sansmaran,* which, a few days before, Jadunandan Sharma had kindly handed me to read before my interview with him. I wrote about my days in Patna after this accident elsewhere, and therefore I do not repeat it here. I could get much support and sympathy from every corner of the Indian society. Karpooriji, who was then in hospital, handed me money with his words of sympathy. Mr. Upendra Maharathi, an artist to whom Dr. Sugimoto introduced me a few months back, provided me accommodation and food in these difficult days. No word is enough to express my thanks to Dr. Sugimoto for his support. The hostel mates of the Hill View Post-Graduate Students Hostel, Magadh University helped me in various ways. I kept contact with a few of them for a long time. In February 1989 Dr. B.L. Sinha, Professor of Geography, invited me to Chapra for my lecture at Rajendra College, Bihar University.

I visited Patna again in March and April 1966. In Patna, I did what I had done at the Archives and Sinha Library before. Gaya in April was terribly hot, and my hostel mates went to their classes in the early morning and in the evening. We took meals twice—about 11 o'clock in the morning and at 10 to 11 o'clock in the evening. We slept in the daytime. My interview with Jadunandan Sharma, a peasant leader and the trusted comrade of Swami Sahajanand Saraswati, was done on 10–11 April 1966. After the interview, Sharmaji served me lemon juice. Due to the heat of Gaya, it was hot juice. But in this gesture, I also felt Sharmaji's feeling of satisfaction for what he had said during the interview. This recording was made possible by the help extended by Dr. Sugimoto. Otherwise it was difficult for me to follow Sharmaji's statements correctly.

However, it took 30 years for me to reproduce this interview in Hindi. It also took 35 years for me to translate Swami Sahajanand Saraswati, *Kisan Sabha ke Sansmaran* into Japanese. These delays were mainly caused by my laziness, but it is also true that it took so many years for me to think of my years in Bihar 1964–66 with some kind of 'objectivity'. The loss of my diary and the heat in Patna of March-April 1966 robbed me of my chance to say thanks to all who helped me, though my feeling of thanks still remains strong. For instance, at Bihiya, I had a nice talk with a young man while I was awaiting the end of the meeting presided by Ramanad Tiwary and he recorded his name and address in my diary or notebook.

I returned to Delhi on 21 April 1966. By this time the ISIS started a new hostel within its site, and I spent a few months in this hostel. I left Delhi for Tokyo on 19 May. On the last evening, I knocked at the door of my neighbour to say goodbye. He had always seemed a 'nonchalant' person. When we were in the same seat of the bus, he liked to hum a tune rather than talk with me. When we were taking really cold baths in the hostel, he did not say anything. However, on that evening, he seemed to be very happy to talk with me till late. His talk covered many issues: world peace, social change in India, the destiny of one Indian historian, and so on. He also referred to the heated atmosphere of discussion developed at the canteen of the ISIS. He said that these enthusiastic scholars paid no heed to two small waiter boys who were talking at the corner of the canteen, and how they should use the money which they just earned. His words reminded me of Delhi observed from the villages in Bihar. Bihar existed in the midst of Delhi too. I have not met him or have not heard about him since then, but I am thankful to him for taking time for me on the eve of my departure from Delhi.

V

The monthly amount of the Government of India Scholarship was Rs. 250, besides the yearly book allowance of Rs. 200, though I had to bear the travelling expenses between India and Japan on my own. I spent my life in India mainly with the hostel food, went to school by bus, and travelled by the Janta Express with the 3rd class coaches only.

When I first applied for the book allowance with the bills for books paid by me, the Registrar of the School immediately responded, saying that all the books which I wanted were available here. There was no need to buy books. Of course, he accepted my application. The Registrar must have been proud of the rich collection at Sapru House Library. Till then I had been quite dissatisfied with the service of the university or other libraries in Japan, and therefore this open-stack library and its nice service made my student life in Delhi fruitful and enjoyable, though its collection was mainly concerned with International Studies, rather than with the contemporary history of India. As for the collection at Sapru House Library, Mr. S. Ansari, who once worked in the library, writes as follows:[8]

> If the size of collection is any measure of greatness of a library, Sapru House Library could never be counted even among the modestly big libraries. For even on the eve of partition of its collection in 1970 (into the Indian Council of World Affairs and Jawaharlal Nehru University), it had a total stock of only 1,20,000 books. What made the library great was the quality of collection and the level of service.

I got competent professional service from the library staff. Not only that, when I planned my first long trip outside Delhi, and needed a small suitcase, one of the staff kindly took me to a shop located at Chandni Chawk. I used this suitcase for two years and half, and lost it in January 1966. Again, I went to the same shop this time for myself. I am still using this suitcase for keeping materials. There was something of a personal touch in the service extended by the library staff.

Before my departure for Japan, Mr. Ansari invited me to a small tea-house near the Jama Masjid of Delhi. Though Delhi in May was terribly hot, that made our friendship permanent. Despite this, I am sorry that I had to trouble Mr. Ansari in the publication of this small collection of our joint work.

A network of my friends in South Asia was expanded from the 1970s to the first decade of the twenty-first century. We hope that readers will understand this seemingly 'unsystematic' collection of essays is, in a sense, relevant to the method of historical studies on South Asia.

In this paper I could not discuss the intellectual encouragement which I received in the 1960s from a small research journal, *Enquiry* published in Delhi, the relations between actors and an audience in Utpal Dutt's drama, *Karror* observed at the Minerva Theatre, Kolkata in December 1965, which depicted the Royal Indian Navy strike of 1946, and my visit to the Fort Museum in May 1964 where I saw a splinter of the Japanese bomb dropped in Chennai in October 1943. As for the third point, Chennai and Kolkata, or Tamilnad and Bengal in 1942–43 never left my memory since then, and in this connection Rajam Krishnan's paper contributes a lot in filling a gap from the side of Tamilnad.

Endnotes

1 S. Seshaiah. 1980. *Land Reform and Social Change in a Japanese Village*, Bangalore: Shiny Publications, pp. 20–1.

2 D.D. Kosambi. 1957. *Exasperating Essays-Exercises in the dialectical Method*, Poona: People's Book House, p. 18.

3 C. Rajagopalachari. 1991. *Jail Diary—A day to day record of life in Vellore Jail in 1920 (sic)*, 3rd edition, Bombay: Bharatiya Vidya Bhavan, pp. 43–4.

4 Anshuman. 2002. *Mritunjaya* (in Hindi), Allahabad: Raka Prakashan.

5 As for Chabbil Das, for instance, see Hansraj 'Ahabar'. 1987. *Mere Sat Janam*-2, (in Hindi), New Delhi, Vani Prakashan, p. 188f.

6 Sho Kuwajima, "A Comparative View of Modern History of Mysore State and Japan", *The Quarterly Journal of the Mythic Society*", January-June 2005, Vol. 96, No. 1-2, and "Reading a Regional History in all-India Context: Munshi Binayak Prasad, *Tawarikh-i-Ujjainiyan* (4 volumes), ibid., January-March 2009, Vol. 100, No. 1.

7 Sho Kuwajima. 2007. 'The Contemporary History which I have seen in India, Bihar and Japan', Hetukar Jha (ed.), *India: Some Crucial Questions*, Darbhanga: Maharajadhiraja Kameshwar Singh Kalyani Foundation;
1996. *Sakshatkar-Bihar ke Kisan Neta Pandit Jadunandan Sharma se Batchit* (in Hindi), Patna: Pratyaksh Prakashan, Preface;
2002. Japanese translation of Swami Sahajanand Saraswati, *Kisan Sabha ke Sansmaran*, Kyoto: Sagano Shoin, Postscript in Japanese.

8 S. Ansari, 'The Rise and Fall of Sapru House Library', *Bulletin of Asia-Pacific Studies*, Vol. 6, 1996, p. 132.

Contributors

Surendra Gopal, Ph.D. (Moscow), taught at the Department of History, Patna University for four decades till he retired in 1996. He has written/edited/translated, a dozen of monographs and published 125 research papers and 200 reviews in national and international journals. His recent publications include *Stepping into Modernity: Patna in the 19th Century*, Khuda Baksh Oriental Public Library, Patna, 2008; *Dialogue and Understanding: India and Central Asia*, Shipra Publications, Delhi, 2005, and *Bihar* (jointly edited with Dr. Hetukar Jha), Kolkata, 2008, under People of India Project. His areas of interest include India's maritime trade in medieval times, Jain society, pre-colonial Indian diaspora, India and Central Asia, and modern history of Bihar.

L.S. Vishwanath, M.A. in History from St. Stephen's College, Delhi, and Ph.D. in Sociology, Delhi School of Economics, University of Delhi, was the Professor and Head of the Department of History, Pondicherry University till his retirement in August 2005. His publications include *Female Infanticide and Social Structure,* Hindustan Publishing Corporation, New Delhi, 2000, and articles in reputed journals and in edited books.

Kazuko Kuwajima was a lecturer, International Buddhist University, Osaka. She translated into Japanese, Sivasankari, *Pirathamarudan Oru Payanam* (in Tamil), Seseragi Shuppan, Osaka, 1995, and Rajam Krishnan, *Manudatthin Maharanthangal* (in Tamil), Sagano Shoin, Kyoto, 2000.

Rajam Krishnan is an eminent Tamil writer. Her novels are based on her intensive study and observation of the exploited and oppressed people, and their struggle for life. Some of her works are translated into Hindi. *Saitril Manidargal* was published as *Mati ke Lal,* Bharatiya Jnanpith, New Delhi, 1991, and *Kurinjee Then* as *Kurinjee Ka Shahad,* National Book Trust, New Delhi, 1996.

Sho Kuwajima is Professor Emeritus of South Asian Studies, Osaka University of Foreign Studies, and the author of *Muslims, Nationalism and the Partition: 1946 Provincial Elections in India,* Manohar, New Delhi, 1998, and *The Mutiny in Singapore: War, Anti-War and the War for India's Independence,* Rainbow Publishers, New Delhi, 2006. He also translated Swami Sahajanand Saraswati, *Kisan Sabha ke Sansmaran* (in Hindi) into Japanese (Sagano Shoin, 2002).